# CULTS

This engaging text introduces readers to the sociology of cults. Covering the history and current state of cult studies, this book includes topics ranging from doomsday cults and new religious movements through to self-help cults, the cult of celebrity, intellectuals, and entrepreneurs. Case studies as varied as David Koresh and the Branch Davidians, the Manson family, and the cult brands of Elon Musk, Andrew Tate and Jordan Peterson are deployed to shed new light on cult formation in the twenty-first century.

Amidst the rise of populist demagogues, the online radicalisation of alienated individuals, and the proliferation of celebrities and gurus with avid followings, cult dynamics are everywhere in society. Yet key urgent questions have not been clearly and concisely addressed: What are cults? Why do they emerge? How are they established and maintained? What is the future of cults, and why are we so fascinated by them? This book explores these questions by tracing the spectrum of cult formation historically and in today's networked media ecosystem.

This accessible introduction to the darkly fascinating world of cults is essential reading for academics and students of sociology, social psychology, religion, politics, business and cultural studies, and anyone interested in understanding the relationship between cults and society.

**Stephanie Alice Baker** is Reader in Sociology at City, University of London, UK. Her research studies self-help and wellness cultures, particularly the role of new media technologies in creating communities and spreading false and misleading health information online. In 2021, she was invited by the UK Parliament to provide evidence on radicalisation, terrorism and extremism, and she continues to assist policymakers in their efforts to reduce and respond to mis/disinformation online. She is the author of *Social Tragedy: The Power of Myth, Ritual, and Emotion in the New Media Ecology* (2014); *Wellness Culture: How the Wellness Movement Has Been Used to Empower, Profit and Misinform* (2022); and co-author of *Lifestyle Gurus: Constructing Authority and Influence Online* (2019).

**Eugene McLaughlin** is Professor of Criminology and Co-Director of the Centre for Criminal Justice and Human Rights at City, University of London, UK. His current research focuses on institutional scandals, 'trial by media,' high profile crimes and cultism. He has also written widely on the politics of policing and the history and development of critical criminology. He is author of *Community, Policing and Accountability* (2023); co-author of *Understanding Deviance: A Guide to the Sociology of Crime and Rule-Breaking* (7th edition, 2016); and co-editor of *The SAGE Dictionary of Criminology* (4th edition, 2019), and *Criminological Perspectives* (3rd edition, 2013).

**Chris Rojek** is Professor of Sociology at City, University of London, UK. His research interests include the sociology of culture, celebrity, leisure and tourism, and social theory. He is the author of *Fame Attack: The Inflation of Celebrity and Its Consequences* (2012); *Event Power: How Global Events Manage and Manipulate* (2013); and *Presumed Intimacy: Parasocial Interaction in Media, Society and Celebrity Culture* (2015). He is also co-author of *Lifestyle Gurus: Constructing Authority and Influence Online* (2019); and editor of *Event Management* (4 volumes, Routledge, 2013).

# KEY IDEAS
*Series Editor: Anthony Elliott*

The Key Ideas series explores major concepts and pressing issues and debates in sociology and the social sciences, from class and sexuality to racism and consumption. The accessible guides offer concise and accessible overviews of core and cutting-edge topics, including class, sexuality, racism and consumption. Each volume is written by a leading expert in the field and uses the latest research findings and cutting-edge approaches from the social sciences to offer critical perspectives and lively, and starkly original interpretations of issues. With new editions redesigned to engage with major global challenges, they offer an assessment of the relevance of ideas for today's world. Books in the Key Ideas series are perfect primers and pre-course reading for students of sociology, political science, economics, psychology, philosophy and geography, as well as approachable introductions to contemporary issues for the interested general reader.

**POSTCOLONIAL EUROPE**
LARS JENSEN

**EXCEPTIONALISM**
LARS JENSEN AND KRISTÍN LOFTSDÓTTIR

**CONSUMPTION**
JOHN STOREY

**SEXUALITY (5TH EDITION)**
JEFFREY WEEKS

**CLASS**
NICK STEVENSON

**HAPPINESS (2ND EDITION)**
BENT GREVE

**RISK (3RD EDITION)**
DEBORAH LUPTON

**RACISM**
ANTHONY MORAN

**CULTS**
STEPHANIE ALICE BAKER, EUGENE MCLAUGHLIN AND CHRIS ROJEK

For a full list of titles in this series, please visit www.routledge.com/Key-Ideas/book-series/SE0058

# CULTS

**Stephanie Alice Baker, Eugene McLaughlin and Chris Rojek**

LONDON AND NEW YORK

Designed cover image: Vector Stock

First published 2024
by Routledge
4 Park Square, Milton Park, Abingdon, Oxon OX14 4RN

and by Routledge
605 Third Avenue, New York, NY 10158

*Routledge is an imprint of the Taylor & Francis Group, an informa business*

© 2024 Stephanie Alice Baker, Eugene McLaughlin and Chris Rojek

The right of Stephanie Alice Baker, Eugene McLaughlin and Chris Rojek to be identified as authors of this work has been asserted in accordance with sections 77 and 78 of the Copyright, Designs and Patents Act 1988.

All rights reserved. No part of this book may be reprinted or reproduced or utilised in any form or by any electronic, mechanical, or other means, now known or hereafter invented, including photocopying and recording, or in any information storage or retrieval system, without permission in writing from the publishers.

*Trademark notice*: Product or corporate names may be trademarks or registered trademarks, and are used only for identification and explanation without intent to infringe.

*British Library Cataloguing-in-Publication Data*
A catalogue record for this book is available from the British Library

ISBN: 978-1-032-37057-6 (hbk)
ISBN: 978-1-032-37059-0 (pbk)
ISBN: 978-1-003-33511-5 (ebk)

DOI: 10.4324/9781003335115

Typeset in Bembo
by KnowledgeWorks Global Ltd.

# CONTENTS

| | | |
|---|---|---|
| 1 | Introduction: Why Cults Matter | 1 |
| 2 | What Is a Cult? The Spectrum of Cultic Influence | 12 |
| 3 | Religious Cults: David Koresh and the Branch Davidians | 32 |
| 4 | Doomsday Cults: The Manson Family | 46 |
| 5 | Celebrity Cults: Ye (Kanye West) | 67 |
| 6 | The Cult of the Entrepreneur: Elon Musk | 82 |
| 7 | Self-help Cults: Andrew Tate | 103 |
| 8 | The Cult of the Public Intellectual: Jordan B. Peterson | 123 |
| 9 | The Future of Cults: From QAnon to the Cult of AI | 141 |
| | Subject Index | 150 |
| | Author Index | 154 |

# INTRODUCTION
## WHY CULTS MATTER

This much is certain. The Liberal Democracies of the West cannot survive. Their leaders are helpless to impose their will upon citizens. Traditional understandings of shared origins, common responsibilities and mutual purpose have atrophied. Reason and Science can only end in knowledge about what is acceptable, not what is true. By turning its back on universal, indivisible, ineffable faith, the West has dug its own grave. Cults have rashly been given the freedom to go forth and multiply. Images have become honeypots of worship. Combustible divisions burgeon. Idols and idolatry have replaced 'Society.'

This is the sum of the doctrinal case against the West made by the Islamic State of Iraq and Syria (ISIS). Western idolatry is portrayed as a death warrant. *Dabiq*, the online magazine of ISIS, legitimates *jihad* against the West by looking to the face of the future. It has no place for cults. 'There will only be the camp of *iman* (faith) versus the camp of *kufr* (apostasy) (Tugendhaft, 2020: 6). *Iman* will prevail. For it is backed by the grace of God. In the territories occupied by ISIS this position was ruthlessly enforced. Apostates were tortured and executed. Dependence upon images was crushed. A variety of means were applied. A *cordon sanitaire* was placed over 'profane' web platforms and exchange. 'Idolatrous' museum and architectural antiquities were destroyed. All of this was done in the name of the caliphate which was studiously committed to become a regime without images. No praxis independent of the mainstream is to be tolerated. *Iman* provides the rule for one and all.

The standpoint of ISIS on *jihad* and *iman* was heavily influenced by the writings of Sayyid Qutb (1906–1966). Qutb believes that the West is beset by a plague of images and idols. It reflects and reinforces a condition that he calls *Jahiliya*: the belief that 'wilful ignorance' seeks to replace God's sovereignty with the sovereignty of man (El-Jaichi, 2022: 113). Qutb's denunciation of the West is partly based upon his two-year study experience in America (1948–1950). Here he came to regretfully conclude that cults have run amok (Qutb 2006). Indiscipline is the order of the day. The main source of his discontent is always faith-based – the belief that the West no longer follows the word and will of God. Nevertheless, he sees contagion everywhere. It is not just the worship of men as gods in literature, film, television, music and art that disgusts him. It is the catalogue of all that goes with it: the loose dress and morals of women; the disrespect shown to marriage and the family; the false allure of money and consumption; the lack of respect shown to the authority of elders; are presented by him as evidence that the West is damned (Qutb, 2006). For Qutb, the remedy is obvious:

> To establish Allah's sovereignty on earth; to arrange human affairs to the true guidance of Allah; to abolish all satanic forces and satanic systems of life; to end the lordship of some men over others, since all men are creatures of Allah and no one has the authority to make others his slaves or to make arbitrary laws for them. These reasons are sufficient for proclaiming *jihad*.
>
> (Quoted in Koylu, 2003: 43)

For Qutb and ISIS, the good society is cult-proof. They therefore immediately diagnose the West as a stricken land. The 'lordship of men over others' in culture, economics and politics is the essence of most Western cults. Their means of recruitment and integration are not uniform. They take two categorical forms. First, the elevation of a messianic leader who accumulates tributes from followers via rituals of devotion and worship. Second, the indirect worship of men and women over others in the shape of commodity fetishism and cargo cults (Miller, 1987: 44, 206; Trompf, 1990; Worsley, 1957). Both entail the sublimation of religious motifs and idioms into secular objects and practices. Qutb and ISIS revile both types of cult as a joint offence against God. In their view, *Jihad* is not about glorifying violence for its own sake. Rather, it decontaminates the world by eradicating cultic images and apostasy, of which the West is perceived to be vulnerable.

We find a similar view in much of the discourse of the Intellectual Dark Web (IDW). The IDW was a term popularised in 2018 by the former *New York Times'* columnist Bari Weiss, to describe 'a collection of iconoclastic thinkers, academic renegades and media personalities,' who hold unorthodox opinions about culture and politics. The loosely held network shares several distinct qualities: rejecting mainstream progressive movements in Western countries, and the emphasis on identity politics, political correctness and cancel culture in higher education and the news media. The IDW comprised figures such as the neuroscientist and podcaster Sam Harris; the mathematician and hedge fund director Eric Weinstein; his brother and sister-in-law, the evolutionary biologists Bret Weinstein and Heather Heying; the psychologist and best-selling author Jordan Peterson; the comedian and commentator Dave Rubin; and the most successful podcaster in the USA, Joe Rogan. The IDW also brought together a series of conservative commentators including Ben Shapiro, Maajid Nawaz and Douglas Murray. 'Feeling largely locked out of legacy outlets,' and in some cases purged from academic institutions, these individuals built their own mass media channels and brands on podcasts, YouTube and Twitter, and in sold-out auditoriums (Weiss, 2018). According to many IDW figures, the West is in decline. For Douglas Murray, a prominent member of the IDW, western history and culture are under threat from within. The 'woke mind virus' is responsible for this moral decline with its radical left, self-righteous ideology infecting western culture and social institutions (see also Teitelbaum, 2021; Murray, 2022; Sedgwick, 2023; Turchin, 2023). What binds both views is their apocalyptic visions of the end of times in which Western society, if it does not wake up, is predicted to invariably meet its demise through cultic indoctrination and attacks from within.

Historically cults have taken many forms. They can vary from intimate relationships between several people to large groups adhering to a hierarchical structure and led by a charismatic messianic figure. In this book we focus on messianic cults. This partly reflects the very extensive and thorough treatment given to the dynamics of commodity and cargo cults elsewhere in the literature

(Berger, 2003; Heath and Potter, 2005). We are also motivated by what we see as the increased profile of cults that threaten the rule of law in Western Society since 9/11. In the aftermath of the September 11 terrorist attacks, much research has focussed on radicalisation and religious fundamentalism in the context of jihadi terrorism (Marwick et al., 2022). During this period, we have also witnessed the mainstreaming of far-right groups in the West – including The Oath Keepers, The Proud Boys and QAnon – many of which are fuelled by evangelical Christianity and conform to typical cult contours. Religious-inspired insurrections are specific to their contexts – the Christian militia groups involved in the January 6 Capitol insurrection are not the same as Al-Qaeda or the military Buddhists in Myanmar. At the same time, there are striking parallels between the ways in which fundamentalist religious extremists and militants justify and enact terrorism by invoking cosmic battles inspired by apocalyptic imaginaries to mobilise violent, fanatical movements (Jürgensmeyer, 2022). In an interesting departure from research on religious fundamentalism, much contemporary cult literature has emphasised that not all cults are religious, with many cults assuming ostensibly secular forms (Lalich, 2017; Montell, 2021).

The standard sociological definition of cults is, 'social enterprises primarily engaged in the production and exchange of novel or exotic compensators' (Stark and Bainbridge, 1985: 172). From this perspective, five characteristics of cult formation can be extracted:

1. *Innovation*: Cults challenge normative order by dissenting and non-conformist beliefs and behaviours.
2. *Challenge*: Innovation takes the form of resistance and opposition.
3. *Freedom*: Challenge is motivated by the desire to free members from the boundaries of a normative order that, at the level of meaning, is experienced as a source of restriction or alienation.
4. *Discipline*: Liberty from restraint is the goal of cult organization and action, but the attainment of this end requires discipline. Cult membership typically involves boundary maintenance. That is, the representation of distance from the normative framework of beliefs and practice by a counter culture

consisting of oppositional beliefs, values, identities, rituals and stigmata.
5 *Leadership*: Cults tend to be defined by group veneration and devotion that is directed towards a charismatic self-appointed leader.

The Oath Keepers, The Proud Boys, QAnon, etc., view themselves as innovators. Bound by their anti-establishment ethos, they challenge the received norms and ideas of mainstream society. Their self-image defines them as champions of liberty. The strong rules of discipline they impose upon members resemble a paramilitary organization in form and content.

Cults have a close relation to religious movements. For example, Christianity began as one of many competing messianic cults. The archetype of the messianic leader is of course Jesus Christ. Cults can also develop from the body of sects within established religions. Qutb became a member of the Muslim Brotherhood and eventually head of its propaganda unit. The Muslim Brotherhood emerged in the 1920s as a fundamentalist Islamic sect dedicated to political activism and social welfare. The activist and welfare aspects of its operations eventually involved the expansion of doctrine to secular political, economic and cultural objectives. Qutb's membership exemplified this in an extremist form. He developed a philosophy of armed struggle against the enemies of *iman* i.e. the elected regime in Egypt. The aim was to purge the government of non-believers (*kafir*) in order to restore Islamic doctrine to its true, original Quranic principles. Because the defence of doctrine shaded into the advocacy of terrorism it was rejected by the majority of Muslims. Qutb was arrested by President Nasser as a totalitarian menace and eventually hanged in 1966. However, his writings are an acknowledged influence on the *jihadi* policies of Al-Qaeda and Hamas (Calvert, 2013; Anari et al., 2017).

Needless to say, while cult organization and practice often incorporates religious motifs and idioms, not all cults are religious or develop paramilitary tendencies. Some offer psychic and somatic healing, compensation for material and spiritual deprivation or occult, ecstatic experience (Stark and Bainbridge, 1985: 172–187). From a functionalist standpoint, cults offer identity and belonging, meaning and purpose, knowledge and enlightenment, leadership and guidance in conditions in which the concept of 'Society' is experienced as either vague and remote (see Chapter 2). As such, cults should not be seen as aberrations. They are constant while proliferating and thriving under certain socio-economic, political and technological conditions.

## SOCIAL MOVEMENTS AND 'THE CULTIC MOMENT'

As the examples of Christianity and Al-Qaeda richly confirm, it is perfectly possible for cults to escalate into full-blown social movements. This is especially true in 'the cultic moment.' That is to say, a time in which general trust relations in the central institutions of society wilts. In these low trust climates, cults offer a base of certainty and a direction of travel that contrasts with the general sense of social *malaise* and transactional diffusion that elsewhere prevails. In the 'post truth' era, these conditions are in the midst of announcing their arrival. There is certainly good reason to maintain that messianic cults are more prominent and disturbing in the current social landscape. From a sociological standpoint, this raises questions about the conditions that have given rise to the current cultic moment. The proliferation of cults and gurus in the twenty-first century is not merely symptomatic of low institutional trust, but the loosening of institutional control over people's lives (Baker and Rojek, 2020). Institutional differentiation is a key characteristic of contemporary western liberal democracies with each institution (e.g. the church, state, science, education, the economy) governed by their own institutional logic (Bell, 1976). The separation of church and state in modernity is symptomatic of what Anthony Giddens termed 'detraditionalisation': the weakening of the grip of tradition over individuals wherein the universal legitimacy that religion once held is replaced by value pluralism (Giddens, 1991). As a result, the authoritative voices that previously governed people's lives lose their control and become more diffuse (Houtman and Aupers, 2007). This loosening of institutional authority encourages or even requires people to seek alternative forms of guidance in a spiritual marketplace that provides choice about whom to follow as a guru or moral compass. This provides a fertile environment for cults to flourish (Baker and Rojek, 2019).

Cults differ from social movements in not possessing the quantitative capacity or means of persuasion to affect fundamental and transformative social change. Their influence is often considerable. However, cultic influence does not translate into a complete, irrevocable capacity to recast normative order like some social movements do. This points to an important analytical difference between social movements and cults. By comparison to cults, social movements are a rare, unusual phenomenon. They are as exotic as truly charismatic leaders who acquire followers on the grounds of being perceived as possessing extraordinary or superhuman qualities (Weber, 1968: 1111–1157). This is not an accident. Genuine social movements and authentic charismatic leaders very frequently only exist in combination. Most commonly, both can be found in highly unstable, tectonically charged situations. When the ground shakes beneath received social, economic, cultural and political regularities, cults come into their own. Notwithstanding this, there is no real reason to follow common-sense and view cults as some sort of volcanic eruption in normative order. It is certainly the case that the cultic moment affords over-capitalisation of cult presence. Dissidence and non-conformity gain scale when *terra firma* suddenly seems unsupportive. This state of disorder opens the stage to groups that were hitherto widely regarded to be peripheral, eccentric and cranky. Despite this, there is no pretext to regard cults as rogue factions in the conduct of life with others, or to hold that the cults that have moved from the periphery to the core inevitably amount to a transformative social movement.

'The cultic milieu' refers to the sum of 'unorthodox and deviant belief-systems together with their practices, institutions and personnel [which] constitutes a unity by virtue of a common consciousness of deviant status, a receptive and syncretistic orientation and an interpenetrative communication structure (Campbell, 1972: 134–135). In stable, high trust times this milieu is confined to the margins of society. Trust here refers to general confidence in the legitimacy of the central institutional arrangement of society. In unusual times, high trust gives way to low trust. With this alteration, the cultic milieu pushes out of the margins. Some components gain sufficient momentum to challenge normative order. Suddenly, what was unorthodox and deviant becomes revolutionary and purposive. The lesson to draw from this is that the common practice of regarding cults pejoratively must be handled with caution. It is groundless to see normativity as all-encompassing or eternal. Normative order never has been, and never will be, universal and unopposed. Society always consists of layers of belief, organisation and practice that are unorthodox and deviant. Cults therefore contradict normative order. The extent to which the antagonism threatens stability is always one of degree. In the words of Antonio Gramsci:

> The people (the sum total of the instrumental and subaltern classes of every form of society that has so far existed) cannot possess conceptions which are elaborated, systematic and politically organized and centralized in their albeit contradictory development. It is, rather, many-sided – not only because it includes different and juxtaposed elements, but also because it is stratified, from the crude to the less crude.
> 
> (Gramsci, 1971: 360)

It is helpful here to borrow Gramsci's reasoning. Cults should be approached as 'juxtaposed elements' rather than abnormal intrusions into the supposed serenity of the normative. They should not be automatically classified as aberrations or threats. It is perfectly valid to submit that cults can be disruptive and destructive. By the same token, it is important to remember that they can also be purgative and constructive.

The book is organised into nine chapters. In a book of this length, no claim is made to be exhaustive. The aim is to explore the conditions that have given rise to the proliferation of messianic cults today and the variety of forms cultic influence assumes through canvassing a variety of historical and contemporary case studies. The cults examined in this book fall into six categories: Religious Cults, Doomsday Cults, Celebrity Cults, Self-help Cults, and the Cult of the Entrepreneur and Public Intellectual. In order to provide a coherent platform for reflection, each type is prismatically examined via a representative case study. Since our focus is upon messianic cults, the following case studies are examined: David Koresh and the Branch Davidians (Religious Cults); Charles Manson (Doomsday Cults); Kanye West (Celebrity Cults); Elon Musk (the Cult of the Entrepreneur); Andrew Tate (Self-help Cults) and Jordan Peterson (the Cult of the Public Intellectual). Of these, it should be noted that only a few are non-American citizens (Elon Musk holds US citizenship but was born in South Africa, Andrew Tate holds dual US and British citizenship, Jordan Peterson is Canadian). The concentration of the world media power in the US provides messianic leaders with the lifeline of a global media network to exchange and frame their outlooks. Cults cannot prosper without communication. This is why the present age of social media expansion is so congenial to cult presence in the world. Ironically, while much research focuses on the role of social media and recommender algorithms in promoting cult like gurus and ideas, legacy media often give oxygen to these figures by amplifying controversial talking points (see Phillips, 2018). Many of the cults focused on in this book are male. This is both an extension of our earlier work on female influencers (Baker and Rojek, 2019; 2020) and an investigation into the social media ecosystem that gives rise to and rewards male gurus in the manosphere, many of whom have established cult followings.

The decline of organised religion provides a fertile space for idols and cult formation. In place of a superhuman deity, celebrity gurus, self-help gurus, tech gurus and intellectual gurus fill the void. The echo of religion explains why cults are held in low esteem. False divinity is idolatry. Voltaire's *Philosophical Dictionary* describes idolatry as a term of 'insult' and 'abuse' (Voltaire, 1971: 258). Under Abrahamic religion, everything that tempts worship to deviate from the one, true God, is objectionable. The religious taboo against cults on the grounds that they align with tendencies towards the worship of idols and idolatry is never far away from secular thinking. However, it wrongly suggests that the intensity of the divisive threat posed by cults is constant. Any historical and social analysis of cults worth its salt recognises that cult formation and duration depend upon what might be called 'the cultic moment'. As the following chapters illustrate, this is a condition in society in which the rule of the beliefs, values and protocols of central authority are destabilised.

## REFERENCES

Anari, H.H., Jalai, R., Ashrafi, A., Ardestani, A.B. and Ghastemabar, S.M.M. (2017). Al-Qaeda understandings from Sayed Qutb's Jihadi Thoughts. *International Journal of Social Science Studies*, 5(7), 79–86.

Baker, S.A. and Rojek, C. (2019). The Belle Gibson scandal: the rise of lifestyle gurus as micro-celebrities in low-trust societies. *Journal of Sociology*, 56(3), 388–404.

Baker, S.A. and Rojek, C. (2020). *Lifestyle gurus: constructing authority and influence online*. Polity.

Bell, D. (1976). *The cultural contradictions of capitalism*. Basic Books.

Berger, A.A. (2003). *Ads, fads and consumer culture: advertising's impact on American character and society*. Rowman & Littlefield.

Calvert, J. (2013). *Sayyid Qutb and the origins of radical Islam*. Oxford University Press.

Campbell, C. (1972). The cult, cultic milieu and secularization. In: Hill, M. (ed.) *A sociological yearbook of religion in Britain 5* (pp. 119–36). SCM Press.

El-Jaichi, S. (2022). Ignorance or sovereignty: the de-territorialization of Jihad in Sayyid Qutb's theo-political vision. *Journal of Political Ideologies*, 27(1), 112–126.

Giddens, A. (1991). *Modernity and self-identity: self and society in the late modern age*. Polity.

Gramsci, A. (1971). *A Gramsci reader*, ed. Gorcas, D. Lawrence & Wishart.

Heath, J. and Potter, A. (2005). *Nation of rebels: counterculture becomes consumer culture*. Harper Business.

Houtman, D. and Aupers, S. (2007). The spiritual turn and the decline of tradition: the spread of post-Christian spirituality in 14 western countries, 1981–2000. *Journal for the Scientific Study of religion*, 46(3), 305–320.

Isaacson, W. (2023). *Elon Musk*. Simon & Schuster.

Jürgensmeyer, M. (2022). QAnon as religious terrorism. *Journal of Religion and Violence*, 10(1), 89–100.

Koylu, M. (2003). *Islam and its quest for peace: jihad, justice and education*. CRVP.

Lalich, J. (2017). Why do people join cults? Ted Talk. Available at: https://www.youtube.com/watch?v=kB-dJaCXAxA

Marwick, A., Clancy, B. and Furl, K. (2022). Far-right online radicalization: a review of the literature. *Bulletin of Technology & Public Life*, May. doi: 10.21428.

Miller, D. (1987). *Material culture and mass consumption*. Blackwell.

Montell, A. (2021). *Cultish: the language of fanaticism*. Harper Wave.

Murray, D. (2022). *The war on the west: how to prevail in the Age of Unreason*. HarperCollins.

Phillips, W. (2018). *The oxygen of amplification: better practices for reporting on extremists, antagonists, and manipulators*. Data and Society.

Qutb, S. (2006). *Milestones*. Islamic Book Services.
Sedgwick, M. (2023). *Traditionalism: the radical project for the restoration of sacred order*. Penguin.
Stark, R. and Bainbridge, W. (1985). *The future of religion: secularization, revival, and cult formation*. University of California Press.
Teitelbaum, B.R. (2021). *War for eternity: the return of traditionalism and the populist right*. Penguin.
Trompf, G.W. (1990). *Cargo cults and millenarian movements: transoceanic comparisons of new religious movements*. De Gruyter.
Tugendhaft, A. (2020). *The idols of ISIS*. University of Chicago Press.
Turchin, P. (2023). *End times: elites, counter elites and the path of political disintegration*. Allen Lane.
Voltaire (1971). *Philosophical dictionary*. Penguin.
Weber, M. (1968). *Economy and society*. University of California Press.
Weiss, B. (2018). Meet the renegades of the intellectual dark web. *New York Times*, 8 May.
Worsley, P. (1957). *The trumpet shall sound*. Macgibbon and Kee.

# WHAT IS A CULT?
## THE SPECTRUM OF CULTIC INFLUENCE

### THEORISING CULTS

Anti-Cult Movement (ACM) authors, most of whom are psychiatrists or psychologists (e.g. Lifton, Langone, Hassan, Singer, Stein), acknowledge that cults exist on a continuum of influence (i.e. the effect a cult has on its members) and a continuum of control (i.e. from less invasive to all-encompassing), rendering them from benign to coercive and extremely dangerous. ACM authors, many of whom are cult survivors (e.g. Steve Hassan and Janja Lalich), focus on dangerous cults that exploit the vulnerable. They have popularised the idea that, regardless of cult diversity, 'dangerous cults' employ manipulative practices to exert harmful levels of control over their recruits. Cults practice deception, with leaders and other group members often lying about the true purpose or goals of the group in order to recruit and retain followers. Cults demand unquestioning self-sacrifice, intense levels of devotion and exclusive commitment to the group, its leader and its creed. Cult membership is maintained through invasive mechanisms of coercion, which include isolating members from the rest of society to exercise control and create a culture of high dependency; generate a surveillance network, premised on a culture of suspicion, to suppress dissent and increase routine control over group members; inculcating a culture of dread with group members told that they will be unable to survive outside the 'safe haven.' ACM authors are committed to exposing the battery of extreme 'mind control' techniques which are used by cults, such as 'brainwashing,' 'love bombing,' 'coercive persuasion' and fear, to destroy independent judgment (see Hassan, 2015; Lalich, 1994; Lifton, 2012; Singer, 1996; Taylor, 2004). As a result of the adhesion processes, cult members are converted into 'deployable agents' who can be depended on to recruit others.

In the late twentieth century, an alternative body of literature emerged that fuses 'cult thinking' with the fields of marketing, advertising and corporate leadership. This literature conceives of successful marketing as a form of 'corporate evangelism,' advising businesses on how to achieve status as a 'cult brand' (Acosta and Devasagayam, 2010; Atkins, 2004; Hanlon, 2006; Ragas and Bueno, 2011; Wittwer, 2014). Hanlon (2006) explains that the most powerful brands create meaning for a 'community of believers' and loyal followers, outlining the brand messages that 'will help every company and marketer capture the public imagination.' Likewise, Atkins (2004) highlights how companies can use 'cult-branding techniques,' such as 'uniqueness' and 'exclusivity,' to achieve 'cult status' and create devoted consumers. This literature mainstreams the idea of 'cult thinking' in the context of branding as an overwhelmingly 'good thing' which satisfies our primordial need for meaning, and to which brands ought to aspire. Consequently, cults are positioned as a 'rich and legitimate source of insight for the creation of brand worship' (Atkins, 2004: xi). The central message put forward by this literature is that 'classic' cultic principles and techniques can also be copied and employed by marketing agencies eager to recruit 'congregants' and convert them to become influential 'true believers.' Once created, a cult brand will enjoy charisma 'that is off the charts,' attracting a devoted global following (constituting the equivalent of a religion) few mainstream brands enjoy.[1] The burgeoning industry of celebrity lifestyle and self-help gurus have also mainstreamed cultish thinking and practices (Baker and Rojek, 2019; 2020).

While this literature has produced valuable insights about the affective dimensions of cults, their psychological proclivities as well as their marketing potential, what is missing from this body of literature is a systematic analysis of the contemporary social, cultural, political, economic and technological conditions that have blurred the lines between the cultish and the mainstream. Literature on cult brands tends to create a simplistic dichotomy between 'benign' and 'dangerous cults,' with cult brands categorised as the former (Ragas and Bueno, 2011) when in reality many cult leaders blur the lines between the two. There is limited academic scholarship that explores how the very marketing techniques used to develop a cult brand can be strategically used by online influencers for destructive ends. In this book we compensate for this neglect, situating the allure and proliferation of cults in the search for meaning in a low trust society characterised by ontological anxieties, uncertainty, confusion, loneliness and meaninglessness. Given that the ubiquity of smartphones and the internet has lowered the barriers to achieving guru status online, our focus is on the rise of messianic cults, enabled by these new technologies. Although cults predate the internet, the ubiquity of digital platforms and social media has facilitated a 'cultic moment' where a multitude of self-styled cults, and 'truthers,' can amplify their message and recruit global 'congregations' searching for meaning in life (MIL) in ways unimaginable in the past. This reflects the condition of low trust that has developed against many of the central social institutions, and the value pluralism that has emerged as a result of the de-traditionalisation processes at work in contemporary western societies. These processes have been summed up by Heelas (1999: 64) as follows: from 'fate' to 'choice' (and associated 'hyper-reflexivity'); from communalism to individualism; from the other-directed to the inner-directed; from authoritative 'basics' to a utilitarian or 'emotivist' culture; from the 'auratic' to the 'anti-auratic'; from exclusivist truth-commitment to relativistic abnegation of judgement; from certainty to uncertainty and risk; from the traditional and the modern to the postmodern.

## THE CULTIC EXPERIENCE

The cultic experience is the articulation of the restless search for meaning in life (MIL), a crucial aspect of being human that we discussed above. Cults satisfy crucial social needs. Among their chief dimensions of seeking are:

1 *Seeking meaning and purpose*: Cults provide their members with a reason to believe and trust in something greater than themselves. They offer the promise of personal redemption and

salvation as a consequence of spiritual 'awakening,' often presented in a compelling Utopian narrative. These narratives frequently employ references to divine authority and transcendental influence. The ideals espoused can take the form of self-improvement, a purpose-driven life, enlightenment and revelation towards the pursuit of truth or a collective shift in consciousness. For seekers, cults provide a sense of meaning, purpose and reenchantment in a highly individualised – and often secularised – society. This emphasis on the spiritual and the transcendent is one of the components that distinguishes the cultic from other collectives. Cults address questions of morality, and the problem of good and evil, that a purely rational and scientific view of the world cannot satisfy. Usually, this belief in the transcendent carries with it an unwavering belief in prophecy and fatalism as an antidote to Sisyphean nihilism, randomness and chaos (Festinger et al., 1956). This commitment to meaning and purpose is accompanied by 'regressive assimilation' – a preference to embrace and honour the 'ancient wisdom' that science and technology has discarded. Strong sentiments of being 'peripheralised' or ignored by established society translate into conspiratorial thinking (i.e. nothing happens by accident, nothing is as it seems, everything is connected – Barkun, 2013) and a social orientation which, on a priori grounds, is indignant. Indignation is fuelled by selective use of folklore and local 'concrete' relations. Similar to the people who espouse it, this knowledge has been rashly 'left behind' by 'progress.' The cultic orientation does not discard 'progress' and 'science' in its entirety. Rather, it adopts a selective approach to science, cherry picking scientific terms and facts and combining them with folklore and concrete 'wisdom.'

2 *Seeking identity and belonging*: Cults offer members an exclusive in-group identity that casts the world into good and bad actors, light and dark forces, those who know the truth and those who do not. An insider–outsider logic is essential to cult formation and practice. Cults generate enemy creation practices to establish group identity and legitimise group practice. High levels of group cohesion and identity are achieved by identifying enemies who threaten the group's beliefs and way of life. Meaning

is relational, with the group defined in relation to a perceived evil or threatening other. The projection of an evil other, and the subsequent division of the world into good and bad actors, is an important aspect of the cultic mind. Being part of the 'in-group' facilitates identity and belonging, and provides friendship and community as a remedy to the loneliness, alienation and polarisation that many experience as a consequence of modernity and individualism that characterises contemporary social life (Bauman, 2005). Cults provide refuge from an ostensibly shelterless world. Cult members coalesce around fear of the outside, such as impending catastrophe and persecutions, that facilitates conspiratorial thinking (in part because the group is closed off from opposing points of view and subsequently lend themselves to affirmative thinking and rigid beliefs, especially online. Normative order is presented as an arena of jeopardy. Through concrete experience and observation, they have turned their back upon it. Narratives of cult belonging rely heavily on imagined ties of resemblance and invented traditions.

3 *Seeking knowledge (gnosis) and truth*: Cults claim to have access to a privileged epistemology and ontology, which provides the assurance of certitude as an antidote to a climate of fear, distrust and uncertainty. This emphasis on moral certainty contrasts directly with the scientific method, which by definition is designed to be tested and accepts that all knowledge is falsifiable. Whereas science encourages questioning and scepticism, cults promote obedience and certitude. Cults are distrustful of institutional authority, established experts and elites, who they see as corrupt and evil. Instead, the cultic privileges stigmatised, proscribed 'outsider' knowledge and folk wisdom (Baker and Rojek, 2019; 2020; Barkun, 2013). Science is implicitly attacked for subjecting the world to quantifiable 'scrutiny,' 'measurement' and 'compartmentalization.' Scientific inquiry has elevated an 'abstract' perspective of the world. Against it, cults emphasise qualitative judgement, concrete relations and lived experience with truth revealed by way of feeling and intuition. Buried in this cultic discourse is commonly a critique of science and technology that has combined to make social life too abstract and

complex. In seeking to reveal or recall 'how things really are' or equally importantly 'could be,' cults privilege tradition and locality over abstract global systems. What cult members are seeking is a process of re-enchantment with the social world. Epistemology in cults is preoccupied with confirming cult faith interests and intolerant of dissenting views. Pure truth elevates lived experience and 'native expertise' (Baker and Rojek, 2020) and the consensus of 'true believers,' but typically remains flexible even when prophesies fail (Festinger et al., [1956] 2013)

4 *Seeking feeling and connection*: Cults establish and sustain intense emotional attachments to cult leaders, members and the ideals of the group by participating in collective rituals and practices. Prayer, meditation, chanting, corroborated singing, dancing, mantras and affirmations provide the foundations of group experience. These ritualised practices establish, and reinforce, commitment to the cult. They cultivate a group consciousness via intense spiritual, ecstatic experiences and heightened collective emotions – what Durkheim ([1912] 2001) termed 'collective effervescence' – that bind the individual to the group and elevate cult members above the everyday to assume a sacred status. Through these rituals, cult members become a universal kinship set apart from the profane. Despite the fact that many contemporary cults appear secular, these spiritual dimensions of experience elevate cult brands from the mainstream, promoting group attachment, conformity and the elimination of questioning and dissent.

5 *Seeking leadership and guidance*: Cults are characteristically directed by visionary leaders, who profess to have exceptional qualities, bestow exclusive 'truths' and convictions and guide members towards 'the light.' The para-social bonds between truth-telling leaders and truth-seeking followers are critical. Charismatic authority is a property that is bestowed by the followers rather than as a characteristic of an individual leader (Weber, 1978: 241). The cult of the leader is related to the presence of circumstances characterised by a high level of distrust, uncertainty and insecurity, creating a strong psychological need for spell-binding leaders and guidance. These psychological

processes are strengthened by the distance from the leader. The further the distance from followers, the more space for followers to project an idealised messianic visionary to guide them in the pursuit of truth and salvation. Cult leadership depends upon repeated success to maintain its grip over followers. The cost of failure is the exposure of leaders as fallible, and therefore unreliable. It is logically possible for cult leaders to maintain authority by denying the evidence of underperformance or failure. However, lack of success is subject to the law of diminishing returns. The more cult leaders fail, the deeper their power base corrodes.

## THE CULTIC MOMENT

Cults emerge in what we refer to as 'the cultic moment,' a period in which society experiences a flourishing of cults and cultic practices. We situate the cultic moment in certain socio-economic and political conditions we refer to as 'low trust society' (see Baker and Rojek, 2019; 2020). Low trust society is a society in which popular faith in the central institutions and political authority that bind society are at a low ebb. To acknowledge the decline of trust in social institutions is not to idealistically purport that there was once a 'golden age' when people had unquestioned trust in institutions. Instead, it is to observe a growing disenchantment with a 'system' that perpetually fails to deliver what it perpetually promises. Today, four key drivers of low institutional trust include:

1 *Unmet expectations due to incompetence or betrayal*: 'Trust has two enemies: bad character and poor information' (Bacharach and Gambetta, 2001: 150). Credibility and confidence in the system is undermined by futile government policies (e.g. wars, recessions), the inability to govern effectively or represent 'the people.' These factors not only facilitate populism, they are seen to reflect both the ability (competence/reliability) and character (integrity/benevolence) of those whom we trust (see Botsman, 2017: 125).
2 *Inequalities of accountability*: Low trust also emanates from the belief that the rules of society are unequally applied and

enforced. Certain people are punished, while others are not. The rules and laws that underpin 'the system' are perceived to enable and sustain inequality. The crisis of institutional trust in this regard is facilitated by a series of trust eroding scandals involving governments, public authorities and corporations (Thompson, 2000; Greer and McLaughlin, 2017). Prominent examples include the 2008 financial crisis, sex abuse scandals involving numerous institutions, Big Food and Big Pharma, the Cambridge Analytica scandal, and the current anti-trust hearings regarding Big Tech. The general public continually feel betrayed by those institutions and leaders who are elected to represent and protect them. The lack of credible institutional responses to these inequities leads to social distrust, collective grievances and conspiratorial thinking.

3 *The decline of shared moral structures and systems of knowledge*: Detraditionalisation, and the associated decline of deference to traditional forms of authority, is accompanied by the rise of individualism, which predominately seeks to protect the interests and rights of the individual. Meaning is no longer found primarily in traditional, shared moral structures, but instead in individuals, microcultures and a culture of consumerism. This new degree of freedom in modernity is encapsulated by the notion of the self as a 'reflexive project' to be continuously worked upon, monitored and developed (Giddens, 1991). Distrust of institutional knowledge and conventional forms of expertise is accompanied by the simultaneous rise of micro-celebrities and influencers on social media, many of whom cultivate cultic relationships and trust through performative displays of intimacy and authenticity (Baker and Rojek, 2019).

4 *The accelerating speed and scale of technological change*: Contemporary social life is characterised by radical uncertainty, disruptive innovation and contradictory realities. Cults prosper from this sense of disruption and ontological insecurity. In a world seen to be ruled by corrupt and covert interests, cults present themselves as redemptive, salvationist alternatives. As a result, it is unsurprising that a cultic moment tends to accompany technological change, from the advent of the printing press, to the internet and AI (artificial intelligence). Technology radically

alters the way trust is understood, earned and maintained (Botsman, 2017). For example, the ubiquity of digital devices and the internet has resulted in an unprecedented volume of conflicting information, which encourages questions about whom to trust and and what to believe. Digital technologies also make it easier to achieve selective exposure, wherein an individual *actively* selects opinions that support their pre-existing beliefs, identity and values.

### *Cults, Subcultures and Microcultures*

A question that emerges when considering the composition and conditioning of a cult is: what is the difference between a cult and a subculture? Subcultures are distinct from mainstream cultures, but not apart from them. They exist within a larger cultural context, differentiating themselves from the mainstream through their interests, tastes and values (Thornton, 2005). These group markers become a form of identity and distinction (Bourdieu, 1984). Cults and subcultures are both anti-establishment, in so far as they resist mainstream culture. But whereas cults tend to arise from the conditions of low trust society (listed above), subcultures position themselves *in relation* to the behavioural codes of the mainstream. This symbolic positioning renders subcultures more akin to 'cult brands,' which 'command super-high customer loyalty and almost evangelical customers or followers who are devoted to them' (Ragas and Bueno, 2011: xxi). Cults, on the other hand, resemble countercultural groups, whose identity is predicated on opposition to, and rejection of, the mainstream (Roszak, 1995). It is no coincidence that the US counterculture coincided with the proliferation of cults in north America (Lalich, 2017). The US counterculture of the 1960s and 1970s was comprised of groups that rejected the conformity and consumerism that characterised post-war American society and those who rejected centralised authority altogether (see Turner, 2010). The countercultural ethos of the time gave rise to the 'back to the land' movement wherein many hippies left suburban life in search of shared consciousness experienced collectively on communes (Baker, 2022). Some communes had a hierarchical structure and clear leadership (see Chapter 4 on Doomsday Cults), however most were characterised by fluid bonds, beliefs and political ideologies (Rorabaugh, 2015). In this regard, while the counterculture facilitated a cultic moment, many countercultural hippies of the 1960s and 1970s shared more in common with subcultural groups like the beats who preceded them (see Ingram, 2020), and a variety of spectacular youth subcultures that flourished in the proceeding generations from the mid-to-late twentieth century: punks, bikers, skaters, skinheads, emos, goths and hip-hop.

This imaginary of youth subcultures is now obsolete. In today's consumer society young people 'have the power to shape and construct new identities, uninhibited and free, unfettered by the (former) restraints of class and social structure, habit or tradition' (Martin, 2009). They can live online and construct personas in a promiscuous global 'supermarket of style,' reflexively 'mixing and matching' and moving between transitory, loosely bounded groupings in the context of fluid identities and shifting sensibilities of style, reminiscent of New Age spirituality. A bewildering profusion of micro-cultural groupings/neo-tribes/nomads/life-style scenes cross-cut or transcend rather than merely express structural positionings (Muggleton 2000). They range from cottagecore to e-girls/boys to steampunk (Kennedy, 2020; Hoskins et al., 2023). In 'this world of shifting images there is no single project, or no one lifestyle, no sense of being to which the individual needs to commit' (Firat and Venkatesh, 1995: 253). As one subculture fizzles out there are many more alternatives.

Microcultures share some similarities with cults in terms of how they establish and maintain group membership. While the word 'cult' tends to connote negative connotations, the term is increasingly used by marketers to develop brand building and customer loyalty (see Chapter 6 on 'The Cult of the Entrepreneur'). There is a large body of literature that has examined fandom in the media and popular culture (Hills, 2000; 2003; Read, 2003; Wanzo, 2015). Much of this literature has focused on celebrity and the 'cult of personality' (Duffett, 2016; Hollander, 2010; Lawrence, 2009). Increasingly, research has examined how the cult of personality pervades global politics (Hassan, 2020; Luqiu, 2016; Reyes, 2020). Researchers have similarly shown that brands resemble some of the characteristics of traditional cults. Montell (2021) demonstrates the power of language to bind the individual to a group or organisation. She contends that cultic influence is not limited to religious or doomsday cults like Jonestown or Heaven's Gate, but occurs in mainstream companies from multi-level marketing schemes like Landmark and Avon to fitness brands like SoulCycle, CrossFit and Peloton. We only have to think about how Apple has cultivated a cult brand with a devoted following. The effects of cultish influence can be substantively different; the former resulting in murder and mass suicide, while the fitness cults listed above can be seen to provide positive social and health effects to their members. What Montell seeks to demonstrate is how both dangerous and ostensibly benign cults use cultish language to recruit, maintain and influence members.

Microcultures can resemble cults in the ways that they cultivate a strong sense of identity and belonging, but they are qualitatively different from the messianic cults that we focus on in this book. While both cults and subcultures involve 'in-group' and 'out-group' boundary distinctions, as we noted above, microcultures tend to be more diverse and fluid and lack the coercive, charismatic leadership and commitment characteristic of cults (Lalich, 2004). The choice, freedom and exit processes involved in most microcultures distinguish them from the conversion, commitment and coercion characteristic of cults.

## *Conversion, Commitment and Coercion*

Whereas an individual's affiliation with a subculture tends to be voluntary, cults involve varying levels of conversion, commitment and coercion. Conversion is typically understood as the process by which a person changes from one religion to another, from one denomination to another, from non-involvement to active religious participation, or an intensification of commitment within an existing religion (Stark and Finke, 2000; Rambo and Farhadian, 2014), becoming what is referred to as a 'true believer.' What is perhaps most consistent across 'conversion studies' is that conversion involves a radical change in consciousness by way of the self and identity (Snow and Machalek, 1984; Iyadurai, 2014). This change can occur gradually or suddenly. The convert's 'universe of discourse' or the way they orient themselves in and understand the world, changes (Snow and Machalek, 1984). This shift results in changes both to the way converts view and tell their life stories (i.e. biographical reconstruction) and, therefore, to the way they make attributions regarding life events. Another consistent aspect of religious conversion is that it has perceptible effects on the outcomes of converts' lives, including changes in their mental health and well-being, changes in their behaviour, and changes in their social contexts and social group memberships (Paloutzian, 1981; Zinnbauer and Pargament, 1998).

Conversion is not limited to religious conversion, but is intrinsic to cultic influence (Lalich, 2017). Even benign cults, such as cult brands, involve a degree of conversion whereby consumers become 'true believers' (Wittwer, 2014). In this book we tend to use the term conversion rather than radicalisation. Research on radicalisation was popularised by studies on terrorism following the September 11 terrorist attacks (see Borum, 2011; Doosje et al., 2016; Maskaliūnaitė, 2015). The rise of far-right groups online in subsequent decades has facilitated growing interest in the concept of radicalisation as an analytical frame to study the process by which individuals are exposed to internet content and then adopt extremist or hateful ideas (Marwick and Furl, 2021). There are several limits of using radicalisation as a concept to study online extremism. First, there is a tendency to assume that to study the radical is to study 'the other,' whereas, as Marwick and Furl (2021) highlight, the roots of far-right ideologies – white supremacy and racism – have an established history in the US and other western countries. Second, while the internet amplifies fringe beliefs, the concept of 'online radicalisation' risks simplifying the causal effects of social media by neglecting the political, economic, and emotional context that contributes to radicalisation. As a result, research on radicalisation tends to simplify the conditions under which radicalisation occurs by presenting radicalisation as a by-product of online exposure (Marwick et al., 2022). Through the various case studies canvassed in this book, we seek to show the multiple possible pathways to radicalisation and the varying ways in which conversion occurs. Some of these conversion practices pre-date the internet (see Chapters 3 and 4 on Religious Cults and Doomsday Cults), while others use a variety of offline techniques and online technological affordances to enhance the adoption of cultic beliefs and ideologies. Together, these case studies show that while the internet does not cause individuals to join cults, it can aid cult formation and commitment.

Many studies seek to identify factors that accentuate the probability of *experiencing* cultic conversion. While some studies focus on the psychological attributes or predictors that render certain individuals susceptible to conversion (Rousselet et al., 2017; Walsh et al., 1995), other research emphasises the ways in which situational vulnerability – how certain situations including the loss of a loved one, a job or a relationship – makes certain individuals susceptible to cultic manipulation and conversion (Curtis and Curtis, 1993; Hassan, 2012). Those who have undergone personal or professional loss are often strategically targeted by cults (Lalich, 2017). Loneliness and a desire for meaning also make one susceptible to recruitment and conversion by virtue of cult members deceptively offering community and friendship (Lalich, 2017). The recruitment process involved in joining a cult can be subtle. It can take time to convert an individual into a 'true believer,' with recruitment often initiated by a trusted friend, colleague or family member (Lalich, 2017). Although the factors that contribute to conversion may vary, conversion is generally conceived as an active process, which questions previous research that conceived of cult membership as the result of 'brainwashing' (Lifton, 2012) or 'coercive persuasion' (Long and Hadden, 1983) inflicted upon an individual. Views of this kind tend to conceive of 'mind control' as involuntary, induced through brainwashing tactics such as social isolation and programming. Most conversions are voluntary and occur in the absence of the sort of confinement and stress experienced by those whose ordeals inspired the model (Snow and Machalek, 1984). Other researchers have posited a 'seekership' orientation that appears to predispose some to conversion. 'Seekers' are more likely to undergo conversion because they are in active pursuit of just such a self-transformation. The idea of 'seekership' evokes the image of one on a journey for personal and spiritual development and meaning. In this case we also see the phenomenon of 'conversion careers' (i.e. the tendency of 'seekers' to move in and out of multiple religious' groups over time).

An alternative 'social drift model' suggests that people convert gradually, even inadvertently through the social relationships which they develop with members of the group. First emphasised by Lofland and Stark (1965) and later by Long and Hadden (1983), this approach gives saliency to affective bonds and connections growing between potential and existing members. Through friendship, attending cult rituals and time with existing members, a person becomes more deeply associated with the groups and begins to adopt the belief system and ways of life. Richardson (1985; see also Dawson, 1990) posit a more active, meaning-seeking movement of an individual who employs his or her will in deciding to convert. They view converts as seekers involved in active and rational searching for a new kind of belief and behaviour, which could bring a benefit to their life. Meadow and Kahoe (1984) argue that factors such as a certain religious background of converts making an encounter with a religious/spiritual solution of problems more plausible; higher suggestibility of converts; presence of paranormal and abnormal signs; etc.

Rambo (1993; 1999) outlines a multi-stage model of conversion, insisting that conversion occurs 'within a dynamic context. The convert is an active agent in conversion and is engaged in a "quest."'Questing relates to motivation and assumes that 'people seek to maximize meaning and purpose in life, to erase ignorance, and to resolve inconsistency' (1993: 46). Questing is an ongoing process that tends to intensify during times of crisis. Although much questing is active, it can also involve a passive openness to external influence:

1 Historical, religious, social cultural and personal context of conversion;
2 Crisis in life of potential convert;
3 Quest, which includes an active agency on the part of the convert in his or her predicament;
4 Encounter with a new religious or spiritual option;
5 Interaction between convert and advocate(s) of new religious or spiritual options, which can include building new relationships, adopting new beliefs and attending rituals;
6 Making a commitment, deciding to become a real member of a new religious community (may involve initialising rituals such as baptism);

7 Experiencing consequences of conversion, including consolidating new identity and commitment, as well as assessing the effect of a new religious option on the convert's life.

Rambo stresses that individual factors and stages are not universal, unidirectional or invariant, but rather interactive and cumulative over time.

Conversion studies suggest that conversion is followed by positive impacts. There is a significant increase of well-being and positive emotions such as happiness, joy, calmness, release. Many converts also shift their sense of responsibility, quality of their relationships, self-esteem, etc. Positive consequences are the termination of drug use, decrease of psychotic symptoms and suicidal thoughts, less distress, less fear of death, greater purpose in life, etc. Some compare the effect of conversion to that of psychotherapy. On the other hand, negative consequences observed after conversion involve non-critical passivity, storm and stress, self-doubts, addiction to a religious leader or other members of the group, family disruption, etc. These contradictory findings give a reason for distinguishing two kinds of conversion: progressive and regressive (Maloney and Southard, 1992) or healthy and unhealthy (Meadow and Kahoe, 1984). Progressive or healthy conversion leads to a positive impact and integration of the convert; regressive or unhealthy conversion results in a negative outcome and dependency. As Rambo notes,

> Conversion is sudden and it is gradual. It is created totally by the action of God, and it is created totally by the action of humans. Conversion is personal and communal, private and public. It is both passive and active. It is a retreat from the world. It is a resolution of conflict and an empowerment to go into the world and to confront, if not create, conflict. Conversion is an event and a process. It is an ending and a beginning. It is final and open-ended. Conversion leaves us devastated – and transformed.
> (1993: 176)

Conversion can be used to describe one's transformation into a true believer in a religious/spiritual ideology, a political cause or even a cult brand. Ragas and Bueno (2011) employ the term 'cult branding' to describe 'the process of actually turning a company, person, place, or organisation into an entity with devoted followers who identify with it and show their commitment in various visible ways' (2011: xxi–xxii; see also Belk and Tumbat, 2005). The proliferation of the term 'cult' in advertising, marketing and popular vocabularies highlights that cults operate on a spectrum or continuum of ethical and undue influence (Hassan, 2015). Ragas and Bueno (2011: xxiii) propose a clear delineation between 'destructive cults,' led by an authoritarian figure, and 'cult brands' in so far as the former is harmful and manipulative whereas the latter is perceived to be harmless and benign. This difference between destructive and benign cults is conceptualised in terms of the cult's form (authoritarian, hierarchical) and effects (destructive mentally and physically). In this book, we take a more critical approach to analysing cult brands, demonstrating that many forms of cultic influence today involve individuals and celebrities who self-brand in destructive and harmful ways. Our focus on messianic cults shows that devotion to a person can slip between harmful and harmless effects whether they wield religious authority offline or status on social media. Cultic influence operates on a continuum from benign to undue influence (Hassan, 2020). In the following chapters, we will critically analyse the spectrum of cult formation and cultic influence in the twentieth and twenty-first century.

## REFERENCES

Acosta, P.M. and Devasagayam, R. (2010). Brand cult: extending the notion of brand communities. *Marketing Management Journal*, 20(1), 165–176.

Atkins, D. (2004). *The culting of brands: turn your customers into true believers*. Portofolio.

Bacharach, M. and Gambetta, D. (2001). *Trust and deception in virtual societies*. Dordrecht: Springer Netherlands.

Baker, S.A. (2022). *Wellness culture: how the wellness movement has been used to empower, profit and misinform*. Emerald.

Baker, S.A. and Rojek, C. (2019). The Belle Gibson scandal: the rise of lifestyle gurus as micro-celebrities in low-trust societies. *Journal of Sociology*, 56(3), 388–404.

Baker, S.A. and Rojek, C. (2020). *Lifestyle gurus: constructing authority and influence online*. John Wiley & Sons.

Barkun, M. (2013). *A culture of conspiracy: apocalyptic visions in contemporary America*. University of California Press.

Bauman, Z. (2005). *Liquid life*. Polity.
Belk, R. and Tumbat, G. (2005). The cult of Macintosh. *Consumption Markets and Culture*, 8(3), 205–217.
Borum, R. (2011). Rethinking radicalization. *Journal of Strategic Security*, 4(4), 1–6.
Botsman, R. (2017). *Who can you trust?: how technology brought us together – and why it could drive us apart*. Penguin.
Bourdieu, P. (1984). *Distinction: a social critique of the judgement of taste*. Harvard University Press.
Curtis, J.M. and Curtis, M.J. (1993). Factors related to susceptibility and recruitment by cults. *Psychological Reports*, 73(2), 451–460.
Dawson, L. (1990). Self-affirmation, freedom, and rationality: theoretically elaborating 'active' conversions. *Journal for the Scientific Study of Religion*, 29(2), 141–163.
Doosje, B., Moghaddam, F.M., Kruglanski, A.W., De Wolf, A., Mann, L. and Feddes, A.R. (2016). Terrorism, radicalization and de-radicalization. *Current Opinion in Psychology*, 11, 79–84.
Duffett, M. (2016). Celebrity: the return of the repressed in fan studies? In *The Ashgate research companion to fan cultures* (pp. 163–180). Routledge.
Durkheim, E. ([1912] 2001). *The elementary forms of religious life*. Oxford University Press.
Festinger, L. Riecken, H.W. and Schachter, S. ([1956] 2013). *When prophecy fails: a classic study*. Simon and Schuster.
Firat, A.F. and Venkatesh, A. (1995). Liberatory postmodernism and the reenchantment of consumption. *Journal of Consumer Research*, 22(3), 239–267
Giddens, A. (1991). *Modernity and self-identity: self and society in the late modern age*. Polity.
Greer, C. and McLaughlin, E. (2017). Theorizing institutional scandal and the regulatory state. *Theoretical Criminology*, 21(2), 112–132.
Hanlon, P. (2006). *Primal branding: create zealots for your brand, your company, and your future*. Simon and Schuster.
Hassan, S. (2012). *Freedom of mind: helping loved ones leave controlling people, cults, and beliefs*. Freedom of Mind Press.
Hassan, S. (2015). *Combating cult mind control: the # 1 best-selling guide to protection, rescue, and recovery from destructive cults*. Freedom of Mind Press.
Hassan, S. (2020). *The cult of Trump: a leading cult expert explains how the president uses mind control*. Free Press.
Heelas, P. (1999). De-traditionalisation of religion and self: the new age and postmodernity. In: Flanagan, K. and Jupp, P.C. (eds) *Postmodernity, sociology and religion*. Palgrave Macmillan.
Hills, M. (2000). Media fandom, neoreligiosity, and cult(ural) studies. *The Velvet Light Trap*, 46, 73–85.

Hills, M. (2003). *Fan cultures*. Routledge.

Hollander, P. (2010). Michael Jackson, the celebrity cult, and popular culture. *Society*, 47(2), 147–152.

Hoskins, K., Carlo Genova, C. and Crowe, N. (eds) (2023). *Digital youth subcultures: performing 'transgressive' identities in digital social spaces*. Routledge.

Ingram, M. (2020). *Retreat: how the counterculture invented wellness*. Watkins Media Limited.

Iyadurai, J. (2014). Religious conversion and personal transformation. In Leeming, D.A. (ed.) *Encyclopedia of psychology and religion*. Springer,

Kennedy, M. (2020). 'If the rise of the TikTok dance and e-girl aesthetic has taught us anything, it's that teenage girls rule the internet right now': TikTok celebrity, girls and the Coronavirus crisis. *European Journal of Cultural Studies*, 23(6), 1069–1076.

Lalich, J. (1994). *Take back your life*. Lalich Center on Cults & Coercion.

Lalich, J. (2004). *Bounded choice: true believers and charismatic cults*. University of California Press.

Lalich, J. (2017). *Why do people join cults?* Ted Talks. Available at: https://www.youtube.com/watch?v=kB-dJaCXAxA

Langone, M.D. *Recovery from cults*. WW Norton & Co.

Lawrence, C. (2009). *Cult of celebrity: what our fascination with the stars reveals about us*. Rowman & Littlefield.

Lifton, R.J. (2012). *Thought reform and the psychology of totalism: a study of 'brainwashing' in China*. UNC Press Books.

Lofland, J. and Stark, R. (1965). Becoming a world-saver: a theory of conversion to a deviant perspective. *American Sociological Review*, 30(6), 862–875.

Long, T.E. and Hadden, J.K (1983). Religious conversion and the concept of socialization: integrating the brainwashing and drift models. *Journal for the Scientific Study of Religion*, 22(1), 1–14.

Luqiu, L.R. (2016). The reappearance of the cult of personality in China. *East Asia*, 33, 289–307.

Maloney, H.N. and Southard, S. (1992) *Handbook of religious conversion*. Religious Education Press.

Martin, G. (2009). Subculture, style, chavs and consumer capitalism: towards a critical cultural criminology of youth. *Crime, Media, Culture*, 5(2), 123–145. https://doi.org/10.1177/1741659009335613

Marwick, A.E. and Furl, K. (2021). Taking the red pill: talking about extremism. AOIR selected papers of internet research. https://doi.org/10.5210/spir.v2021i0.12207

Marwick, A., Clancy, B. and Furl, K. (2022). Far-right online radicalization: a review of the literature. *The Bulletin of Technology & Public Life*, May. doi: 10.21428

Marx, K. (1977). *Capital*. Lawrence & Wishart.

Maskaliūnaitė, A. (2015). Exploring the theories of radicalization. *International Studies: Interdisciplinary Political and Cultural Journal* (IS), 17(1), 9–26.

Meadow, M.J. and Kahoe, R.D. (1984). *Psychology of religion.* HarperCollins.

Montell, A. (2021). *Cultish: the language of fanaticism.* Harper Wave.

Muggleton, D. (2000). *Inside subculture: the postmodern meaning of style.* Berg.

Paloutzian, R.F. (1981). Purpose in life and value changes following conversion. *Journal of Personality and Social Psychology*, 41(6), 1153–1160.

Ragas, M.W. and Bueno, B.J. (2011). *The power of cult branding: how 9 magnetic brands turned customers into loyal followers (and yours can, too!).* Currency.

Rambo, L.R. (1993). *Understanding religious conversion.* Yale University Press.

Rambo, L.R. (1999). Theories of conversion: understanding and interpreting religious change. *Social Compass*, 46(3), 259–271.

Rambo, L.R. and Farhadian, C. (eds) (2014). *The Oxford handbook of religious conversion.* Oxford University Press.

Read, J. (2003). The cult of masculinity: from fan-boys to academic bad-boys. In Mark Jancovich and Antonio Lazaro Reboll (eds) *Defining cult movies: the cultural politics of oppositional taste* (pp. 54–70). Manchester University Press.

Reyes, A. (2020). I, Trump: the cult of personality, anti-intellectualism and the post-truth era. *Journal of Language and Politics*, 19(6), 869–892.

Richardson, J.T. (1985). The active vs. passive convert: paradigm conflict in conversion/recruitment. *Journal for the Scientific Study of Religion*, 24(2), 163–179.

Rorabaugh, W.J. (2015). *American hippies.* Cambridge University Press.

Roszak, T. (1995). *The making of a counter culture: reflections on the technocratic society and its youthful opposition.* University of California Press.

Rousselet, M., Duretete, O., Hardouin, J.B. and Grall-Bronnec, M. (2017). Cult membership: what factors contribute to joining or leaving? *Psychiatry Research*, 257, 27–33.

Singer, M.T. (1996). Therapy, thought reform, and cults. *Transactional Analysis Journal*, 26(1), 15–22.

Snow, D. and Machalek, M. (1984). Sociology of conversion. *Annual Review of Sociology*, 10, 167–190.

Stark, R. and Finke, R. (2000). *Acts of faith: explaining the human side of religion.* University of California Press.

Taylor, K. (2004). *Brainwashing: the science of thought control.* Oxford University Press.

Thompson, J.B. (2000). *Political scandal: power and visibility in the media age.* John Wiley & Sons.

Thornton, S. (2005). *Club cultures: music, media, and subcultural capital.* Polity.

Turner, F. (2010). *From counterculture to cyberculture: Stewart Brand, the Whole Earth Network, and the rise of digital utopianism.* University of Chicago Press.

Walsh, Y., Russell, R.J. and Wells, P.A. (1995). The personality of ex-cult members. *Personality and Individual Differences*, 19(3), 339–344.

Wanzo, R. (2015). African American acafandom and other strangers: new genealogies of fan studies. *Transformative Works and Cultures*, 20(1).

Weber, M. (1978). *Economy and society*. University of California Press.

Wittwer, D. (2014). *The phenomenon of cult brands: the role of culture in building strong brands*. BoD – Books on Demand.

Zinnbauer, B.J and Pargament, K.I. (1998). Spiritual conversion: a study of religious change among college students. *Journal for the Scientific Study of Religion*, 37(1), 161–180.

# RELIGIOUS CULTS
## DAVID KORESH AND THE BRANCH DAVIDIANS

### WHAT IS A RELIGIOUS CULT?

Before coming to the questions of why religious cults arise and how they operate, it is worth beginning with an important distinction between *sects* and *religious cults* (Bainbridge and Stark, 1979). A sect is a formation within a church that diverges from the weight of convention. In Troeltsch's classic study, sects are religious splinter groups. They are oriented to purify the beliefs and practices of the mainstream that are deemed to have strayed from the true doctrinal path (Troeltsch, 1931). Elsewhere it has been contended that sects constitute a type of 'epistemological authoritarianism' (Wallis, 1975: 93). That is, they claim to possess access to content and standards of scriptural reading that are veridical. Typically, they proceed to the conclusion that religious doctrine and practice needs to be revised and recast. Sects are therefore co-dependent with scripture. They believe themselves to possess, or are near to possessing, the ultimate truth. Upon this basis they hold that it is legitimate to dispel the authority of the curators of theology who disagree with them. For example, Luther's attack on the papacy in the 16th century deplored what he took to be the excessive luxury and ornamentation of Catholic hierarchy. He was not alone. In the same century, reformed theology cleaving to the supreme value of austerity in belief and practice, was the project of non-confirming religious potentates such as the Swiss theologian Huldrych Zwingli and the Frenchman John Calvin (Gordon and Trueman, 2021). Sects are unstable entities. In the classic literature they are presented as having a dualistic destiny. Either they will be co-opted by the mainstream, or they will transform themselves from a dissenting branch into a new denomination (Niebuhr, 1929).

Religious cults develop by means of doctrinal divergence that is combined with opposition to secular dominant belief and value systems, be they cultural, political, economic, racial, ethnic or an equivalent social dimension of secular distinction. Religious cults are not the result of determinate doctrinal *fissure*, (as is the case with sects), but of a *coalescence* involving multiple points of resistance (Richardson, 1979: 159–160). That is, they pull together a variety of critical positions on authority in general and synthesise them. Two things should be noted. First, the synthesis is often highly provisional; and second, it borrows and applies religious motifs and idioms. In the condition of stable social order these positions are mostly confined to the fringes. The term 'cultic milieu' has been used to describe this territory (Campbell, 1972: 122). The concept refers to a conjunction between 'the cultural underground,' comprising 'unorthodox science,' 'alien and heretical religion' and 'deviant medicine' (Campbell, 1972: 121–122). Campbell maintains that cults 'tend to have undefined boundaries, fluctuating belief systems (and) rudimentary organizational structures' (Campbell 1972: 121). Their public profile is bound up with Media representation. A sect becomes a religious cult when the article of faith that confers doctrinal identity spills over into grievances and nostrums born and applied in the areas of politics, culture, economics, race, ethnicity, etc. A cult becomes a sect when an article of doctrinal difference is allowed to stand for the basis of recruitment and membership.

It is scarcely to be doubted that the cultural milieu is a constant in society. However, in the condition of low trust society, fringe groups cease to remain underground. Their beliefs, rituals and identities are no longer hidden from plain sight. A cultic moment is born. All of this helps to crystallise the key difference between religious sects and cults. Sects are usually issue-based. Invariably, doctrinal divergence is the salient issue. Religious cults are based in a *condensation* of issues. Doctrinal divergence often functions as the gateway to enlist political, cultural, economic, ethic and other group forms of complaint. Mention of the issue of condensation raises a significant analytical technical issue. With regard to sects, experience and meaning can generally be referred back to doctrinal meaning. Conversely, in respect of cults, organisation and practice often require analysis to allow for *slippage* and the *over-determination* of meaning.

Inevitably, the questions of doctrinal difference, slippage and meaning poses the puzzle of what constitutes 'religion.' The two institutional prerequisites are creed and clergy. The term 'creed' refers to a system of faith-based belief and practical, honorific obligations, attached to a presence that is worshipped as ultimate and divine (Coppleston, 1974). Veneration and personal obeisance to the transcendent, sacred 'Other' is rewarded with salvation (Thrower, 2022: 202). Divine presence is understood to surpass human perception and consciousness and to ultimately determine the structure and types of agency in which human affairs are conducted. At the most basic level, the term 'clergy' refers to the custodians of creed. That is, the trained, specialised personnel who orientate their lives around the tasks of formally perpetuating the divine presence. Sects usually respect transcendence and custodial precedents. In contrast, religious cults sublimate doctrinal precedents and condense them with consecutive beliefs and practices that are secular in form and operation. Both sects and religious cults respect salvation as an axial principle of recruitment, membership and practice.

## WHY DO RELIGIOUS CULTS EMERGE?

Concretely, there are three main routes to religious cult formation. First, cults accumulate around perceived manifestations of magic and the uncanny. For example, the Marian cult remains prominent and significant. The apparitions of the Virgin Mary recounted by the French girl Bernadette Soubirous in 1858 continue to attract scores of pilgrims to Lourdes. In 1933 Bernadette was beatified by Pope Pius XI. The glass coffin where her mummified body reposes in the chapel of the *Espace Bernadette Soubrious Nevers*, is a Roman Catholic shrine. Likewise, the apparition of the Virgin Mary that appeared to three shepherd children in 1917 remains honoured by pilgrims to Fatima, which is indeed now seen as a sacred site (Jansen and Notermans, 2010: 71). Second, cults assemble around a political or cultural cause that assumes mystical or semi-mystical overtones. For example, QAnon sprang from a political and cultural reaction against encroaching precarity. The de-industrialization and loss of working-class jobs in the American 'Rust Belt' produced widespread social unrest. Behind this was a long standing resentment against elites. In QAnon, secular, political and cultural conspiracy messaging is overlain with religious motifs from Christian and Hebrew scripture to proclaim 'the apocalypse' and the imminent removal of 'the world-ruling cabal' (MacMillen and Rush, 2022). The third form of cult formation refers to the transformation of a religious sect into a cultural and political *cause célèbre*. For example, historians now see the sectarian mysticism of the seventeenth-century New England salvationist Anne Hutchinson (1591–1643), as a forerunner of the feminist challenge to patriarchy (Westerkamp, 2021). Another, more recent example, is the cult around the Branch Davidian sect of Waco. It is the Waco case that is selected here for further examination as a case study. The Waco siege (February–April 1993) provides an especially dramatic example of what is called here 'cultification,' i.e. the process whereby a numerically small sect directed by a charismatic leader becomes a national/global *cause célèbre*. It is a particularly apposite case study, for it clearly demonstrates the axiomatic importance of mediatisation in cult formation.

## HOW ARE RELIGIOUS CULTS ESTABLISHED AND MAINTAINED?

The Branch Davidian sect is a prophetic, apocalyptic religious formation based in Waco, Texas. It is a splinter group from the Seventh-day Adventist denomination which itself has roots in the nineteenth-century Millerite movement. The latter refers to a religious group that emerged around the prophecies of the American Baptist farmer, lay preacher and biblical chronologist William Miller (1782–1849). Miller prophesised the 'Second Coming' of Christ and the purification of the earth by fire. The date he set was firm. The Second Coming was scheduled for 22 October 1844. The absenteeism of divine manifestation on the appointed day led to the event being memorialised as 'The Great Disappointment.' The Seventh-day Adventist Church arose from its ashes. It is a radical millenarian denomination that preaches strict observance of the sabbath and the impending return of Christ. It enforces rigid rules of abstinence with respect to the wearing of jewellery and cosmetics; the consumption of meat, coffee, tea, alcohol; and participation in theatre, dancing, gambling and card-playing. It regards itself to be the true, 'remnant' religion, i.e. a Christ-centred Bible church, based upon prophetic disclosures in the *Book of Revelation*. It accuses the present day custodians of Abrahamic faith to be guilty of apostasy. Hence, the self designation, 'remnant religion,' i.e. the true faith. The Branch Davidians (1929) developed out of a rift with Adventism. The sect's founder, Victor Houteff, published a declamatory book, *The Shepherd's Rod* (1930), that submitted a list of doctrinal and custodial faults in the Adventist Church. The text offered a revisionist reading of chapters 54–66 of *Isiah* to proclaim the need for reformation. Houteff reaffirmed the doctrines of sabbath-keeping, the impending end of the world and the Second Coming. However, critically, he added the conviction that the main responsibility of followers was to identify 'the 144,000' decreed in scripture to be the redeemed of the earth who would also be the foundation of the 'New Kingdom' of Christ. Preparatory to the Second Coming, a 'last judgement' of the dead and the living to determine the elect was necessary. Houteff declared that this was already underway in heaven. In a controversial breech with the Adventist creed, he affirmed that the New Kingdom will be physically located in the Holy Land (specifically Israel) (Newport, 2006: 76–111). The Adventist hierarchy condemned the contents of *The Shepherd's Rod* as heresy. Houteff was subject to disfellowship in 1930. He relocated to Waco, Texas where he acted as a theological researcher, writer and self-appointed pastor of what he initially called 'Davidian' teaching (named in support of what he regarded to be the Biblically ordained restoration of the new 'Kingdom of David' in Israel). After Houteff's death in 1955 this group became the 'General Association of Branch Davidian Seventh-day Adventists' or 'Branch Davidians' (1955). An eventful period of leadership ensued. Houteff was succeeded by his wife, Florence. She continued the sabbath-keeping and apocalyptic tradition, culminating in her prediction of a new date for 'the end of times' and the Second Coming: 22 April 1959. When, once again, this culminated in disappointment, leadership passed to Benjamin Roden. He and his family enlisted in the sect as organisers in the late 1940s (after themselves undergoing disfellowship from the Seventh-day Adventists). Upon his death in 1978, his wife Lois took over. Thence, following a highly public power struggle, her volatile and violent son George assumed control (1984). In 1988 David Koresh replaced him.

To this point the Branch Davidians mostly conformed to the conventional meaning of a religious sect. That is, they held fast to the principle that they were chosen and protected by God by virtue of their doctrinal integrity. Oneness with God meant obedience to the absolute, necessary prophecies of the Second Coming. Branch Davidians regarded themselves as God's servants. Under the complex and conflicted personality of Koresh they moved from a strict doctrinal base to a platform that mixed doctrine with secular points of resistance, i.e. to a religious cult The crux of this was Koresh's revelation that being instruments of God required taking steps to overthrow Babylon and expedite the Second Coming. Branch Davidians could no longer wait for the end of times. They had to become more instrumental in preparing for the transition and building the road to the New Kingdom. Among Branch Davidians, Koresh became revered not only as a leader, but as the tool of divine purpose.

Koresh's given name was Vernon Howell. He was from a broken home with a history of violence. He suffered from dyslexia and was not academic. He dropped out of high school at 16 and became a carpenter, mechanic and odd job man. He also became a born-again Christian and joined the Southern Baptist Church. Following a rift with them, he switched to the Seventh-Day Adventist church. He was eventually expelled after seeking to take an underage girl as his bride. In 1981, when he was 22, he moved to Waco and joined the Branch Davidians. During a visit to the site of what would be the New Kingdom in Israel, he claimed to have been visited by seven angels who revealed to him that he possessed prophetic power and was the new 'light of the world' (Newport, 2006: 183). In 1984 he married a 14-year-old member of the Waco congregation, Rachel Jones. He also took to increasingly impassioned, idiosyncratic readings of scripture. In time, Koresh asserted that he was chosen by God for a special mission. Specifically, he preached that the figure on the white horse who is come to destroy Babylon, described in Revelation 19:11, is none other than himself.

Incontestably, his identity, image and conduct became increasingly messianic. Under his leadership, the extra-mural content of preparing to do God's will included the likely necessity for members of the congregation to eventually bear arms. With retrospect, this was prefigured in Koresh's rise to power. By the mid-1980s

George Roden was increasingly hostile to the messianic turn taken by Koresh. A leadership struggle ensued. This culminated in Roden accusing Koresh of committing arson in an administrative building on the Waco estate. Koresh was expelled at gunpoint. He fled to East Texas with his supporters. Here he began to recruit new followers. In 1987 he tried to gain armed control of the Waco estate. Roden was shot in the gunfight, but survived. Koresh was tried for attempted murder, but was acquitted on grounds of mistrial. With Roden incapacitated, Koresh became the Branch Davidians' leader. In 1990 he legally changed his name to David Koresh. He adopted 'David' from the Hebrew bible. David is the slayer of Goliath, and third king of Israel. 'Koresh' was taken from Isaiah 45:1, and refers to the 'anointed' one' (messiah) who subdued Babylon. The Christian name and surname are therefore both associated with heroism and warrior status (Arnold, 2023: 104–105).

As leader, Koresh's messianism developed along three extra-mural fronts: procreative, combative and interrogative. Part of the revelations given to him consisted of his God-given duty to procreate. As designate prince of the New Kingdom, he required offspring to be active and prominent in the 144,000. Accordingly, Koresh presented having sex with female members of the sect as legitimated by doctrinal necessity. His quest to procreate took two stages. First, he claimed and exercised the right of sexual congress over unmarried Branch Davidian women. Eventually he extended the prerogative to the married (Newport, 2006: 199). The topic of where divine mission ends and sexual exploitation begins remains an open question in assessments of this side of Koresh's leadership style (Newport, 2006: 199–204). On the combative front, he presided over the accumulation of a significant arsenal consisting of semi-automatic/automatic weapons, ammunition, grenades and night vision equipment in the Waco compound. After the siege, federal officials claimed that Koresh had assembled more than a million rounds of ammunition (Toobin, 2023: 82). During his period as leader Koresh justified weapons stockpiling as a measure of prudent self-defence against the forces of Babylon. Conversely, the authorities regarded the sheer scale of the arsenal as a clear and present danger. The interrogative side of Koresh's tenure took the form of back peddling on the general isolationism of the sect and engaging with selected political and cultural controversies of the day. The main areas of activity were secular liberty, free speech and individualism. In terms of concrete issues, this boiled down to gun ownership, the absolute right of privacy with regarded to personal behaviour and what is now called 'originalism,' i.e. the ascendance of the Constitution as the means of conflict resolution. Thus, religious free speech was justified by the First Amendment, just as the Second Amendment was invoked to justify the stockpiling of weapons and ammunition.

Koresh's support for originalism directly paralleled his belief in the authority of prophecies in the Book of Revelation.

With hindsight the procreative, combative and interrogative features of Koresh's leadership constituted an explosive tinder box. Sexual licence with minors in the estate fuelled allegations that Koresh was a paedophile. In fact, the Texas Department of Human Services questioned Koresh about allegations of actual or potential child abuse. No evidence was found (Newport, 2006: 202–203). However, the rumours persisted. After the siege, psychiatric research into surviving Davidian children concluded that Koresh had engaged in grooming and the sanctioned sexual abuse of children (Perry and Szalavitz, 2017). On 28 February 1993 the climate of suspicion surrounding possible juvenile sexual relations with Koresh and the stockpiling of weapons and ammunition precipitated the Bureau of Alcohol, Tobacco, and Firearms (ATF) to authorise agents to arrest him and investigate Branch Davidian behaviour. A patrol of over 70 personnel entered the grounds of the Waco estate in cattle trucks, with aerial support from three National Guard helicopters. A frontline unit attempted to serve search and arrest warrant by effecting a 'dynamic entry.' The tactic is now widely regarded to have been a grave error (Newport, 2006: 249–254; Guinn, 2023). Entry was blocked. A gun fight erupted. Four ATF agents and six Branch Davidians were killed. Additionally, both sides suffered multiple gunshot casualties. The FBI rapidly assumed management of the crime scene. The attempted forced entry escalated into a major incident, covered by national and global media, that lasted for 51 days.

From the outset, the Waco siege developed into a media frenzy. Camera crews relayed events from outside the estate. Broadcasters reported radio-com exchanges between Koresh, other Branch Davidians and FBI negotiators. This resulted in several conflicting consequences. The public connotations of the Branch Davidians with isolationism, religious mania and paramilitary extremism were enhanced. In particular, the perceived messianism of Koresh emerged as the defining feature of the crisis. Against this, militia, gun rights and originalist groups defended the Waco besieged as exponents of free speech, gun ownership and the right to privacy. The government response was condemned as draconian. It was taken to confirm the punitive, repressive mind set of the purported secret power elites running society. As for the view within the Branch Davidian compound, Koresh spoke for the overwhelming majority. He proclaimed the siege to be the fulfilment of the textual prophecies in the Book of Revelation. The AFT and FBI were defined as the agents of Satan. For a long time Koresh had been preaching that the overthrow of Babylon would require a bloody battle. Without demur he preached that death would very likely be the price to be paid for victory. He commended this to the congregation. By the grace of God, death would necessarily result in rebirth and the greater glory of the Second Coming. As already noted in this chapter, the Millerite movement prophesied that the end of the world and purification would come by fire. It was surely not accidental that the siege was ended (on 19 April 1993) by what is now widely accepted to be a self-inflicted fire (Newport, 2006: 278–280). Seventy-five Branch Davidians died, including 28 children and Koresh himself.

## WHAT IS THE FUTURE OF RELIGIOUS CULTS?

On the question of the future of religious cults, most pioneering sociological contributions have been in agreement (Becker, 1932; Martin, 1966). They judged such cults to be invariably of weak integration and ineffectual agency. For these reasons they were typically classed as ephemeral. Howard Becker traced this back to the foundation of cult formation that he took to consist of 'purely personal ecstatic experience' (Becker, 1932: 627). The controls over recruitment and obligations of membership are presented as secondary. He proceeded to propose that their 'loose texture' and 'amorphous' assembly means that they will inevitably be 'transient' (Becker, 1932: 627). Nearly three decades later, the prominent British sociologist of religion, David Martin, concurred (Martin, 1966).

According to him, 'the fundamental criterion of the cult is therefore individualism' (Martin, 1966: 124). This is a strange proposition. For individualism appears to pre-empt group membership which is usually seen today as a hallmark of cults. Martin emphasises individualism because he wants to accentuate the foundational importance of personal ecstatic experience in cult assembly. There is no mistaking Becker's use of the adjective 'purely personal.' Martin seeks to build upon it by describing 'the fundamental criterion' of cults as 'individualism.' Upon this basis Becker and Martin are able to classify religious cults sociologically as essentially ephemeral phenomena.

This posture now seems obsolescent. With hindsight it wrongly privileges *subjective experience* over *cult organization*. Personal ecstatic experience is conceptualised as meaningful, but necessarily disjointed and lacking group direction. Religious cults are inevitably 'loosely textured' because subjective ecstatic experience is not readily communicable, nor is it easily repeated. These pioneering contributions therefore understood religious cults to be atomised and temporary. Conversely, the Waco case teaches two important lessons: first, given certain external preconditions, a messianic leader is perfectly able to externalise and package ecstatic experience into a durable, all-encompassing feature of group mentality and action. Second, media concentration carries the possibility of elevating a group to become a symbolic rallying point for a variety of otherwise inconsistent secular protest groups and movements. Messianic leadership and media concentration combine to accelerate the cultification of groups, i.e. national/global identification and inflexible support that is beyond rational accounting practice.

To go into each lesson in a bit more detail, *prima facie*, the Waco group was indeed outwardly 'amorphous' and 'ineffectual.' It consisted of members having diverse accredited educational attainments (including graduates) and mixed race and nationality (45 were people of colour and while Americans comprised the majority, there were citizens from the UK, Canada, Australia, Israel, Mexico, Jamaica, the Philippines and New Zealand among their number) (Newport, 2006; Barkun, 2007: 118). Between the days of the founding father Victor Houteff and the leadership of Koresh, it languished as a semi-isolated sect. From a free speech standpoint, it was theologically antithetical to the values of the surrounding society.

Threatened armed struggle was not on the agenda. The Second Coming was in the hands of God. In terms of interstitial cohesion the main converting factor that made the Branch Davidians an oppositional unit to the rule of law was leadership. Under Koresh, the Branch Davidians were regimented around messianic force that was ultimately portrayed as having divine approval (and hence could not be justly challenged). Koresh translated his ecstatic revelations of action and apocalypse into group identity cards. Strict rules of membership were introduced to divide insiders (believers) from outsiders (non-believers). The abstract foe of scripture – 'Babylon' – was distilled into the concrete, material threat of government. Koresh left the doctrinal base intact. However, in terms of group superstructure, his secular vision proliferated an oppositional outlook among the Waco Branch Davidians that was far more antagonistic to the outside world than his predecessors. He absorbed selective elements of cultural, political, economic and originalist controversy into the Branch Davidian self-image.

If the siege had never happened the Branch Davidians would, very likely, have been permitted to continue on the margins of society. For generations it had been tolerated in Texas as a numerically insignificant, eccentric, essentially benign sect. Under Koresh, the procreative element of his leadership regime attracted the interest of the Texas Department of Human Services. But the investigation by state officials came to nothing. The procreative side of the sect did not precipitate decisive state action. Rather, it was the interrogative, and particularly, the *combative* elements of Koresh's leadership standpoint that acted as the tipping point. The stockpiling of weapons and the increasing use of Second Amendment/freedom rhetoric was perceived as a risk to the rule of law. It is now generally agreed that the so-called 'dynamic entry' strategy of the AFT was bungled (Newport, 2006; Guinn, 2023). A major unintended consequence was to turn the Branch Davidians into a national and global media phenomenon. For many, the Waco siege became a symbolic totem of liberty against state tyranny. In the course of this, the doctrinal foundation of the Branch Davidians was largely eclipsed. In the process of cultification, Waco crystallised into a freedom cult. It attracted diverse disaffected factions concerned with white power, racial 'replacement,' Second Amendment rights, police brutality, state corruption, economic exploitation and other anti-government issues. Media concentration transformed the Branch Davidians from sectarian dissidents into renegade combatants. During the siege this was exploited and heightened by Koresh. He played a cat and mouse game with FBI negotiators, promising in one breath to bring the stand-off to an end, only to revoke the promise in the next breath. Koresh was keenly aware of the value of publicity. He ruthlessly sought to engineer the siege to encourage media framing to communicate it as a showpiece for doctrinal privilege and individual freedom against state oppression. In the event, he was far more successful in turning Waco into a symbol of the fight for freedom than a beacon of doctrinal integrity.

Cultification does not simply have immediate, short term consequences that may be quickly forgotten. It also builds a legacy. Two years after the Waco siege came to a violent end, the Alfred P. Murrah Federal Building in Oklahoma City was destroyed by a car bomb (1995); 168 people were killed, including 19 children. At the time, the media portrayed the assailant, Timothy McVeigh, as a lone, pathological drifter. The criminal investigation unearthed evidence that supported a conflicting narrative. McVeigh was a veteran of the Iraq war. He had a long-standing history of attending gun fairs and obsessing over right-wing literature, notably, the notorious white supremacist cult novel, *The Turner Diaries* (MacDonald, 1978). In 1993 McVeigh drove to Waco to distribute extremist propaganda and witness the siege at first hand. The Oklahoma bombing was timed to commemorate the second anniversary of the violent climax of the Waco siege (Toobin, 2023). McVeigh saw the Murrah Building bombing as a revenge attack against what *The Turner Diaries* characterised as the villainous state. The symbolic force of Waco did not end with McVeigh's execution in 2001. It continues to be an inspiration for the far right and populist extremists. In the notorious storming of the United States Capitol Building (6 January 2020), representatives from 'The Proud Boys,' 'Oath Keepers' and 'QAnon' referred to Waco as a government assault against free speech, individualism and gun rights. In addition, it was hardly accidental that Donald Trump selected Waco as the venue for the first rally of his 2024 Presidential campaign (26 March 2023). By way of evidence, it should be noted that Trump's speech deployed the 'weaponisation' of the state and characterised his presidential campaign as 'the final battle.' The resonance with the Waco confrontation could scarcely be missed.

In the foregoing account it was observed that messianic cult leadership requires 'certain external preconditions' to prosper. Chief among these is 'the cultic moment.' The cultic milieu is a constant in the social landscape. It is therefore present at any time and any place under all imaginable power regimes. For the most part, it is containable, i.e. it is confined to the fringes of society. What makes the cultic milieu an active, mobile disruptive influence upon social order is 'the cultic moment,' i.e. a concatenation of economic, social, political and cultural conditions that fuels general sentiments of low trust in the established societal authority structure. In conditions of low trust, the liberal welfare democracies are particularly vulnerable to a reaction from religious cults. This is because their authority is based upon the rational-legal rule of law. When this rule is widely perceived as malfunctioning, religious cults are well placed to challenge liberal-democratic authority with faith-based solutions to the ills of society. Religious cults are always based in belief systems that are not subject to rational accounting practice. This does not mean that their dissent from social order is irrational or incommunicable. Unemployment, inflation, racial strife, hostility to bureaucratic procedure proliferate an all-encompassing sense of system malfunction. They spread the seeds of dissent and disruption. Koresh certainly exploited the post-Vietnam sense of malaise in America to build the interrogative repertoire of his leadership. Media concentration on the siege supplied the missing ingredient that ensured national/global cultification. Koresh and McVeigh did not live to witness the social media age. They lacked the technical means to build bridges between renegade silos and transcendentalist factions. Today, the world wide web supports ample information highways not only to accumulate low trust in established authority but to forge cultification around systems of belief that are beyond rational accounting practice. In the study of cults, the religious cult is unlikely to be the sociological backwater that pioneering contributors predicted. *Contra* Becker and Martin, the opportunities for unregulated information exchange, allied with the challenges that liberal democracies face to overcome the low trust malaise, are likely to raise the profile of religious cults in the social landscape.

# REFERENCES

Arnold, J.P. (2023). Did David Koresh plagiarize Cyrus R.Teed? *Nova Religio*, 26(3), 101–115.

Barkun, M. (2007). Appropriated martyrs: the Branch Davidians and the radical right. *Terrorism and Political Violence*, 19(1), 117–124.

Becker, H. (1932). *Systematic sociology*. John Wiley & Sons.

Campbell, C. (1972). The cult, cultic milieu and secularization. In: Hill, M. (ed.) *A sociological yearbook of religion in Britain*. Vol. 5 (pp. 119–136). SCM Press.

Coppleston, F. (1974). *Relgion and philosophy*. Gill and Macmillan.

Gordon, B. and Trueman, C. (eds) (2021). *The Oxford handbook of Calvin and Calvinsim*. Oxford University Press.

Guinn, J. (2023). *Waco: David Koresh, the Branch Davidians and a legacy of rage*. Simon & Schuster.

Jansen, W. and Notermans, C. (2010). From vision to cult site: a comparative perspective. *Archives de Sciences Sociales Des Religions*, 55(151), 71–90.

Lawson, R. (1996). Seventh-day Adventist responses to Branch Davidian notoriety. *Journal for the Scientific Study of Religion*, 34(3), 323–341.

MacDonald, A. (1978). *The Turner diaries*. National Vanguard Books.

MacMillen, S.L. and Rush, T. (2022). QAnon: religious roots, religious responses. *Critical Sociology*, 48(6), 989–1004.

Martin, D. (1966). *Pacifism: an historical and sociological study*. Routledge & Kegan Paul.

Newport, K. (2006). *The Branch Davidians of Waco*. Oxford University Press.

Niebuhr, R. (1929). *The social sources of denomination*. Henry Holt.

Perry, B. and Szalavitz, M. (2017). *The boy who was raised as a dog and other stories from a child psychiatrist's notebook* (3rd edn). Basic Books.

Richardson, J. (1979). From cult to sect: creative eclecticism in new religious movements. *Pacific Sociological Review*, 22, 139–166.

Thrower, J. (2022). *Religion: the classic theories*. Edinburgh University Press.

Toobin, J. (2023). *Homegrown: Timothy McVeigh and the rise of right-wing extremism*. Simon & Schuster.

Troeltsch, E. (1931). *The social teachings of the Christian churches*. Macmillan.

Wallis, R. (1975). Scientology: therapeutic cult to religious sect. *Sociology*, 9(1), 89–100.

Westerkamp, M. (2021). *The passion of Anne Hutchinson: an extraordinary woman, the puritan patriarchs, and the world they made and lost*. Oxford University Press.

# DOOMSDAY CULTS
## THE MANSON FAMILY

In this chapter we will discuss the making of a notorious doomsday cult. The Manson family are part of a group of cults that believe in apocalypticism, including both those that prepare for 'End Times' and those that decide on homicidal or suicidal behaviour to accelerate 'End Times' (Lifton, 1999). We use the Manson family as a case study to explain how doomsday cults emerge and function. The chapter describes the cultic milieu that enabled Charlie Manson to transition from paroled ex-con to charismatic hippy guru and finally apocalyptic '*Helter Skelter*' prophet. We will then consider the distinguishing features of Manson's 'guru' playbook, recruitment and conversion practices, the family's group dynamics and detail the crisis-driven shift from 'sex, drugs, rock 'n' roll and mysticism' to preparing to bring down '*Helter Skelter*,' Charlie Manson's version of the Apocalypse. The concluding section considers the powerful cult *mythos* that continues to mark out the Manson family out from other cults. It is the Manson family, along with Jim Jones, David Koresh and Shoko Asahara, that defines the very idea of a nightmarish 'End Times' cult directed by a master manipulator. Prior to Charlie Manson and his 'family' of followers the concern about cults in the USA had focused on 'the cult of personality' and fringe 'new religious movements' (Lifton, 1961; Beam, 1964; Lofland, 1966).

To construct this case study we have drawn upon news media reports, documentaries, films and the following books that have published about the Manson family (Atkins, 2005; Bugliosi and Gentry, 1974; Cooper, 2018; Didion, 1979; Emmons, 2019; Faith,

DOI: 10.4324/9781003335115-4

2001; Fromme, 2022; Guinn, 2013; Lake, 2016; Melnick, 2018; Meredith, 2018; O'Neill, 2019; Sanders, 1971; Watson, 2019; Wells, 2009; Wiehl, 2018).

## WHAT IS A DOOMSDAY CULT?

Doomsday thinking, or 'endism' is not just limited to cults. Many groups work within an 'End Times' framework believing that an apocalyptic global event (supernatural, natural, man-made or extra-terrestrial) will destroy humanity (Thompson, 1999; Eco et al., 1999). Most mainstream religions operate within an afterlife narrative that includes 'End Times.' Among Christians, for example, probably the most well-known and powerful eschatological vision is contained in the New Testament's Book of Revelation. This vision includes the Second Coming of Christ, the epic battle between Christ and the anti-Christ, the establishment of a new Jerusalem and Final Judgement Day. For many Christian fundamentalists, 'End Times' also includes 'the secret rapture,' the cataclysmic moment when, before the Second Coming, 'true believers' will be saved from the nightmarish period of tribulation presided over by the anti-Christ (Frykholm, 2004; Pagels, 2012; Sutton, 2014). The accompanying message for all true believers is that it is vital to be vigilant as 'End Times' could engulf humanity at any time. A recurrent problem for 'true believers' is accounting for a prophesy of 'End Days' that fails to materialise (Festinger et al., 2009).

The 'Doomsday Clock,' which was created in 1947, warns about 'how close we are to destroying our world with dangerous technologies of our own making. It is a metaphor, a reminder of the perils we must address if we are to survive on the planet' (*Bulletin of the Atomic Scientists*). Founded by Albert Einstein and the scientists who invented the atom bomb, the original focus was to warn about the threat of mass annihilation. More recently its remit has been expanded to include the risks posed by climate change, disease and malevolent technologies. The clock's hands are moved towards or further away from midnight based on analysis of the degree of threat at a given time. Midnight is the moment of self-destruction. In January 2024 the clock was set at 90 seconds to midnight, due to Russia's invasion of Ukraine and the heightened risk of nuclear escalation being added to the escalating mix of threats. Acting as a 'canary in the coal mine,' the clock is intended to press governments to take urgent internationally coordinated action to save the future. Climate crisis activists such as Greta Thunberg also deploy 'endist' thinking to alert the world to the forces that are bringing the earth to the brink of extinction (Thunberg, 2022). 'Apocalypticism' reverberates in popular entertainment culture with innumerable novels, films and television dramas such as *The Road*, *Mad Max* and *The Last of Us*. They furnish us with a variety of post-apocalyptic imaginaries of what will be left of humanity after time has ended. In 'real life' there has also been a notable upsurge in people adopting a survivalist lifestyle, with radicalised 'preppers' stockpiling extensive resources and learning how to 'live off grid' in anticipation of imminent societal collapse (Kabel and Chmidling, 2014; Mills, 2019; Rushkoff, 2022). In November 2023 doomsday prepper Elon Musk launched Tesla's new 'Cybertruck' boasting that it would be 'apocalypse-proof.' A specially assembled audience was informed by Musk that 'The apocalypse can come along at any moment, and here at Tesla we have the best in apocalypse technology.'(Folk, 2023).

When it comes to doomsday cults, Lifton (1999) argues that they are led by a megalomaniacal guru who has a vision of an apocalyptic event or series of events that will destroy the world in the service of a new beginning. The vision can be either of the guru's own making or be synchronised with apocalyptic thinking in the wider cultic milieu. Members of doomsday cults, who have already been subjected to intensive socialisation, are radicalised as they prepare for 'End Times.' This is particularly the case if, as the 'chosen ones,' they will be the only survivors in the post-apocalyptic world. There is, however, a significant difference between predicting that the end is nigh and attempting to force 'End Times' (Lifton, 1999). Cults who foresee 'End Times' concentrate on making ready for what is inevitably going to come to pass and are alert to signs that the end is nigh. Cults who are 'mandated' to hasten 'End Times,' through the use of homicidal and/or suicidal violence, are of course giving themselves a much more devastating role. In deciding on when, where and how to accelerate the apocalypse these cults cross the threshold to the point where there is no going back (Lofland, 1966; Lifton, 1999; Kaplan and Marshall, 1996). Even if a cult leader prophesies 'End Times,' it still requires followers to not only embrace the prophesy but to bring it to pass.

## WHY DO DOOMSDAY CULTS EMERGE?

It is important to note from the outset that nobody joins a doomsday cult and 'a cult is not created, *de novo*, destructive but *becomes* destructive' (Bohm and Alison, 2001: 133). The warning signs of a cult *becoming* truly destructive include:

- The group isolating itself (geographically, socially or cognitively) from the rest of society and drawing ever sharper boundaries between 'them' and 'us,' 'godly and satanic,' 'good and evil';
- The group's belief system being defined as the ultimate, unquestionable 'Truth';
- Members becoming totally dependent on the absolute leader for their understanding of reality with intensifying degrees of internal control and important decisions about members' lives being made for them by an inner circle;
- Leaders claiming divine authority for their actions and their demands, pursuing a totalist goal in an unwavering manner, becoming more paranoid in their understandings of the group and the outside world and foretelling the group's role in an apocalyptic event or series of apocalyptic events.

(Barker 1989: 137; Lifton, 1999: 202–207).

For a variety of internal and external reasons, some of these groups begin to tip over, entering a quickening doomsday mindset, embracing violence, building defensive psychological and physical fortifications and acquiring weapons (Bohm and Alison, 2001; Hall, Schuyler and Trinh, 2000). In so doing they have decided to impose their reality on the outside world.

As part of the imposed reality, the guru becomes the ultimate bastion against the evil of defilement, the central figure in the world purifying apocalyptic narrative. The narrative is considered the only certainty in an otherwise unknowable future. That is the guru becomes the scared agent of a divine plan for all encompassing purification.

(Lifton, 2019: 7)

## HOW IS A DOOMSDAY CULT ESTABLISHED AND MAINTAINED?

Thirty-two-years-old Charlie Manson, a career criminal, was paroled from a prison near Los Angeles on 21 March 1967. He had been in and out of correctional institutions since he was a teenager. Given the degree of his institutionalisation, Manson should have been out of time with the youth quake convulsing American society. However, during his incarceration he claimed that he had studied Dale Carnegie's self-help strategies, Eric Berne's 'transcendental analysis,' and Dianetics and Scientology; participated in group therapy and psychiatric sessions; read Robert Heinlien's sci-fi novel *Stranger in a Strange Land*, and absorbed 'what was happening' in popular culture. Fascinated by Beatlemania, he also practised constantly on his guitar, singing and writing songs (Emmons, 2019).

Upon release Manson decamped to Berkeley and then Haight-Ashbury, the centres of the hippy counterculture. He found a 'convict's dream' making the most of the free-for-all cultic milieu consisting of

> the entire collection of subcultural currents that had been building up in the US during the previous decade. Acid music. Dope. Sexual freedom. Turn on, tune in, drop out. The politics of free. Peace rallies. Provos. Guerilla theatre. Communes. Long hair. The concept of underground superstar. Astrology. The occult. Underground newspapers. Crash pads. Dayglo art.
>
> (Sanders, 1971: 35)

This cultic milieu was vital to Manson's re-invention as a hippy 'guru.' He quickly transitioned in looks and attitude, managing to 'tune in' and pass for one of the multitude of wannabe male rock stars and/or freak gurus and mystic cult leaders drifting round southern California. Busking and preaching he managed to acquire a small group of female admirers, describing himself as 'the Gardener' who was tending to his 'flower children.'

His followers, colloquially known as the Manson family, all presented similar accounts of the life-changing moment they encountered Charlie Manson. They were captivated by the charismatic Manson and relished the attention that he conferred on them.

- 'When he focused his attention on you, he made you believe there was no one else in the world. He had an uncanny sensibility bestowed upon him' (Lake, 2018: 129);
- 'he charmed – in the original sense of the word – and he had an uncanny ability to meet a person and immediately psyche him out, understand his deepest fears and hang-ups, his vulnerabilities. It was as though he could see through you with the all encompassing eye of God … his eyes were hypnotic' (Watson, 2019: 80);
- 'something happened that has no explanation … I experienced a moment unlike any other … it was beyond human reality' (Atkins, 2005: 5);
- 'Charlie only had to look at us and we would do anything he wanted … *anything*' (Kasabian, 1971).

Victor Bugliosi, the prosecutor in the Tate-La Bianca murder trial, declared that Manson 'had a quality about him that one thousandth of 1 per cent of people have. An aura, "Vibes," the kids called it in the Sixties. Wherever he went, kids gravitated toward him' (Hedegaard, 2013). According to Family members, Manson was defined not just by his extraordinary power to hold in thrall anybody he met but his access to the truth, powers of 'postulation' to make things happen and the ability to read and change minds (Nielsen, 1984). Followers took it for granted that he was 'the Messiah come again.' And Manson repeatedly pushed the idea that he, the 'Son of Man,' was indeed the reincarnation of Jesus Christ, something that was 'revealed' to him in a prison.

> This is not something that I've wanted. It happened one day in prison. The Infinite One just came into my cell and opened up my head. He showed me the truth. But I did not want it. I cried and yelled 'NO, NO, NOT ME.' But he showed me the truth.
>
> (Atkins, 2005: 105)

One of his most powerful drug fuelled sermons included a re-enactment of how he had died on the cross to save all of them (Lake, 2016: 283).

As the group took initial form first in San Francisco, on numerous road trips in a ramshackle school bus and in the communes and 'borrowed' houses where they crashed in Los Angeles and finally Spahn Movie Ranch, their desert ranch headquarters, followers became part of a surreal 'family' (Sanders, 1971: 101). Manson's playbook yoked together his prison education, Timothy Leary's counter cultural message of 'turn on, tune in, drop out,' scripture and his grifter sensibilities (Leary, 1999; Emmons, 2019: 97–98). It all started harmlessly enough. As the followers smoked dope and dropped acid, Manson preached what would have already been a familiar liberationist sermon:

- swapping their old 'up-tight' lives for a trip on the 'Magical Mystery Tour';
- rejecting the world that had rejected them;
- divesting themselves of material possessions and living a communal life;
- renouncing their previous identity and their family and friendship networks;
- pushing aside their conventional 'hang ups' and shedding feelings of guilt;
- killing their egos through 'ceasing to exist' as individuals;
- erasing their past and relinquishing the future in order to live in the eternal 'Now';
- understanding that happiness could come from any direction so long as they opened themselves up to every experience.

From the outset, 'sex, drugs, rock 'n' roll and mysticism' were central to both the metamorphic process being used to liberate family members and to attract new recruits. The women were socialised by Manson to accept as normal sexual exploitation by him, the other men in the family and any other men that he directed them to. They were not allowed to use contraception and were required to accept collective child-rearing practices. The 'sacred' powers of drugs, particularly LSD, were used to facilitate transition to a higher state of existence and communality. Ecstatic states were manufactured by tripping on LSD, group singing, dancing, encounter games and sex orgies. Manson's obsessive song writing and singing played a critical role in family bonding and grooming, providing members with their own exclusive soundtrack and in-group language (Montell, 2021). He also sold his followers on the dream that they were part of the Californian folk rock protest music scene and that he was destined to be more famous than the Beatles, the Beach Boys and Dylan. His fame as a singer-songwriter would generate the wealth needed to finance the family's alternative lifestyle and disseminate his 'new truth' gospel. Much of the family's time was spent working towards his manifest destiny (Watson, 2019).

This belief was reinforced when the family began to mix with Beverly Hills-Hollywood based musicians, most notably Dennis Wilson, of the Beach Boys, with whom they lived and who introduced him to the Byrds producer Terry Melcher and arranged recording sessions for the 'guru' whom he referred to as 'the Wizard.'

> Manson could share a table at the *Whisky à Go Go* with someone like record producer Terry Melcher, Doris Day's son. Where members of the Beach Boys could hang with members of the 'family,' who, in turn, rubbed shoulders with the Straight Satans biker gang. Where beautiful people could throw parties and have no idea who was taking LSD by the pool. Where everyone was looking for a guru, no background checks required.
> (La Ganga and Himmelsbach-Weinstein, 2019)

Followers were groomed to believe in nothing but loyalty to the family; solve any problems that the family faced; confront their fears, including death; forage for and take whatever they needed; distrust and exploit anyone who was not part of the family; understand that an attack on one family member was an attack on all family members.

On the move and under Manson's 'practice makes perfect' tutelage, family members discovered how to neutralise any inhibitions about surviving through hustling, stealing and dealing. Followers also learned to be possessive of Manson, the mystical heart of their lives. They competed for his attention and were rewarded with additional affection. The women were bombarded with examples of how they could not survive outside of Manson's protection. Traumatic experiences of the menacing, chaotic outside world, including rape, reinforced dependency on Manson and other family members. Manson stated that because the women's defences were easier to break down, it was simpler for them to 'cease to exist' (*Rolling Stone*, 25 June 1970) (Felton and Dalton, 1970). Signalling public devotion to Manson was expected. Humiliation was the punishment for those who did not accept his sermons as gospel truth or failed to follow through on his directives. This was psychologically disorienting for followers who, at the same time, were being told by Manson to think for themselves and be game for anything. Constant shifts in the interpersonal power dynamics amongst family members as well as trying to keep up with Manson's churning mind were also disorienting.

Family members regulated each other and socialised new recruits into this evolving group mindset (Beck, 2016; Lake, 2019; Watson, 2019). The first group of female followers had a central place in the interpersonal power dynamics of the group: in proselytising, conversion, grooming, and integration processes. As the family's star recruiters they zeroed in on other young women whom they thought would fit in with the family. Potential members were seduced and sold on their joyful 'born again' lives with 'Charlie.' From Manson's perspective it helped if new recruits were 'smart,' came from affluent homes and/or had connections. Looking instantly familiar in their dishevelled 'hippy chic' appearance, the Manson women also projected a strong sense of sisterhood that provided reassurance that their family was a safe space. Their strong personal ties to Manson and sister wives relationships with each other also normalised the group's sexual rites of passage.

The image of young, sexually liberated, fun-loving hippy women was also deployed to attract men who were deemed to have practical skills or who were wealthy or influential male benefactors, particularly in the entertainment industry. For example, Beach Boy Dennis Wilson was befriended after a chance encounter with two members of the family who were hitchhiking into Los Angeles.

Manson assured the relatively few men in the family that, subject to accepting his Alpha status and acquiring more young women, they would be treated like kings by 'Charlie's girls' (Watson, 2019).

During 1969 there is general agreement that the mood changed within the makeshift commune at the Spahn Movie Ranch (Lake, 2016: 294). Manson's guru playbook shifted to strengthening his hold on and radicalising the thoughts and actions of his inner circle through conjuring up an apocalyptic vision, based on biblical prophesies regarding 'End Times' and the Beatles' *White Album*.

The radicalisation was two-fold in nature. First, Manson ratcheted up the collective paranoia by pointing to an assortment of 'Piggy' establishment enemies who were threatening their way of life. 'Piggies' ranged from the police to contacts in the Los Angeles music industry, including Dennis Wilson, who were failing to deliver on Manson's recording career. Second, Manson schooled the family on how to interpret the Beatles *White Album*, particularly the 'Piggies,' 'Helter Skelter' and 'Revolution #9' tracks, as a warning of a violent racial reckoning that was 'gonna come down fast.' Manson's 'End Time's' prophesy was first spun at a family gathering on New Year's Eve 1968 at Myers Ranch, near California's Death Valley (Watson, 2019).

He prophesised that '*Helter Skelter*' would be sparked by a group of enraged blacks committing atrocious murders in the wealthy neighbourhoods of Los Angeles and other cities 'writing "pigs" on the walls … in the victims' own blood.' These crimes would, in turn, produce total chaos, unleashing retaliatory white violence in black neighbourhoods. These attacks would be exploited by Black Muslims and the Black Panthers, provoking a devastating civil war between racist and non-racist whites over the shocking treatment of blacks. At the end of the civil war, Black Muslims and the Black Panthers would re-emerge to wipe out the surviving whites. Manson reassured the family that they would be the only exception. As the elect they would safely wait out the race war in a 'Bottomless Pit' underneath Death Valley where they would never age. The family, the last remnants of white civilisation, would emerge from their subterranean refuge as the beneficiaries of the war. Incapable of handling the reins of power, the victorious blacks would ask Manson to rule over them. His 'End Times' masterplan decreed that the family would be in control of the post-apocalyptic world (Bugliosi and Gentry, 1974; Watson, 2019).

Immersion in Manson's apocalyptic reading of the *White Album* and preparing for '*Helter Skelter*' re-energised the family, transforming it, in effect, into a doomsday cult caught up in an 'End Times' project: moving back and forth between Los Angeles and their desert bases; mapping out escape routes to their final Death Valley hide-out; stockpiling a cache of firearms and provisions; assembling 'dune buggies'; stealing jeeps, motorbikes and trucks for their evacuation; and participating in survivalist 'kill or be killed' and 'creepie crawly' training sessions. A rig of lookout posts were set up on Spahn Movie Ranch and Hell's Angels were enrolled to provide extra protection for the family. Parts of the ranch began to resemble a fortified encampment. Manson ratcheted up their criminal endeavours to finance the final preparations for '*Helter Skelter*', generating dangerous run-ins with other criminals and activating law enforcement attention.

According to family members, in the summer of 1969 there was a dramatic shift in Manson's 'End Times' project, from siege mentality planning to signalling to his stalwarts that they would have to hasten the end.' Manson admitted that they were up 'against a wall of fear and paranoia' (Emmons, 2019) as a result of: the fallout from botched drug deals, the arrest of family members as well as his fury about what he viewed as deliberate attempts to sabotage his record contract and rip off his music. Without his agreement, the Beach Boys had reworked one of his songs, 'Cease to Exist,' into 'Never Learn Not To Love' without crediting him. The song appeared on their 1969 album *20/20*.

Manson's 'snapping point' (Conway and Siegelman, 2005) was reached in early August 1969.

> All I could focus on was 'What the fuck is happening here? One by one this fucked up society is stripping my loves from me. I'll show them! They made animals out of us – I'll unleash those animals – I'll given them so much fucking fear, the people will be afraid to come out of their houses.'
>
> (Emmons, 2019: 199)

A hand picked 'murder squad' was dispatched to 'do what blackie didn't have the energy or the smarts to do – ignite *"Helter Skelter"* and bring in Charlie's kingdom' (Watson, 2019). Manson suggested that the murder squad 'hit some rich pigs' (Emmons, 2019; Watson, 2019) in an exclusive neighbourhood that they were familiar with. The killings should be as 'witchy' as possible and in order to turn '*Helter Skelter*' into a reality and make it look as if they were the work of the Black Panthers.

American society was convulsed by the killing spree which claimed seven victims, most notably Sharon Tate, the pregnant actress and wife of director Roman Polanski. Tate's blood was used to write the word 'Pig' on the front door of her luxury home at 10050 Cielo Drive in Benedict Canyon where she was murdered with four of her friends. The next night, at a Los Feliz residence, another exclusive Los Angeles enclave, Leno and Rosemary LaBianca were murdered. The phrases 'Death to Pigs,' 'RISE' and 'Healter Skelter,' (misspelled) were scrawled in their blood at the crime scene. The gruesome details of the murder spree immediately captured the Californian news agenda, as did wild speculation as to the motive for their deaths. The murders

> had everything to intrigue and titillate a public that seems to relish the personal failings of the same people that it worships as demi-gods. Pictures of the stunning blonde actress pushed immediately pushed Jacqueline Onassis and Elizabeth Taylor off the cover of every pulp magazine ...
>
> (Roberts, 1969)

The superconductive nature of the murders and the fact that the unknown killers remained at large stoked a panic about home invaders wreaking Satanic 'porno-violence' in Los Angeles' exclusive neighbourhoods. In anticipation of further violent home invasions, there was an immediate rush for guns, watchdogs and private security (Sanders, 1971; Bugliosi and Gentry, 1974; Emmons, 2019).

The murders remained unsolved until the autumn of 1969 when the police arrested Charlie Manson and members of his 'family.' It took some time for police to connect them to the two nights of killings. The breakthrough came when one of the family, Susan Atkins, who was being held on other charges, boasted to her cellmates about her role in the killings. Upon arrest, the accused were characterised in the news media as a drug crazed 'mystic cult' or nomadic 'hippy cult' known as 'Satan's Slaves' or 'tribe of nomads' or 'hippy clan' or 'hippy commune' called 'the family' who practised 'a kind of witchcraft' and were under the mesmerising control of Charlie Manson, a bearded, 'wild eyed' Rasputin-like leader or 'guru' who called himself Jesus Christ and the Devil (*Daily Telegraph*, 3 December 1969).

> The cult to which they belong is an anomaly even in the offbeat hippy world, and beyond its members' proclivity for violence. The men wear long hair but the women crop theirs short and they identify with no-one but their own clan group.
> (*Washington Post*, 3 December)

The Tate-LaBianca murder trial, which began in June 1970, was the longest, most expensive and freakish in US history.

> It had famous rock 'n' roll stars like Dennis Wilson of the Beach Boys, who briefly housed the so-called Manson family; it had the appeal of the Wild West; it had the bass drum of the 1960s, with its sexual liberation, its love of the outdoors, its ferocity and its open use of drugs. It had the hunger for stardom and renown; it had religions of all kinds; it had warfare and hometown slaughter; and it had it all in a huge panorama of sex, drugs and violent transgression … [it] ripped aside the veils of Hollywood and inflamed the world's interest.
> (Sanders, 2019)

Charlie Manson stood accused of masterminding the murders by unleashing his 'killer zombies' to slaughter at his behest. Vincent Bugliosi, the prosecutor, told the court:

> The family that lived on Spahn Ranch was … nothing more than a closely knot band of vagabond robots who were slavishly obedient to one man and one man alone, their master, their leader, their God, Charles Manson. Within his domain, his authority and power were unlimited. He was the dictatorial maharajah, if you will, of a tribe of bootlicking slaves who were

only too willing to do his bidding for him. Charles Manson's family preached love but practices cold blooded, savage murder. Why was that so? Because Charles Manson, their boss, ordained it ... He controlled everything that they did on a day-to-day basis. He even controlled their sex lives.

(Bugliosi and Gentry, 1974)

The trial was characterised by frenzied media coverage of both the details of the murders and the accused, constant disruptions, abuse of legal process, death threats and peculiar happenings. Members of the jury listened to the Beatle's *White Album* to familiarise themselves with the songs claimed to have influenced Manson and his followers. They were tutored on the mind-altering effects of drug taking. At one stage defence lawyers requested that John Lennon be called to give evidence. It was also alleged that the family had drawn up a 'kill list' of Hollywood stars.

Manson and his three co-defendants, Susan Atkins, Patricia Krenwinkel and Leslie Van Houten, who were mobbed by the news media, 'regarded the trial as a mockery and behaved accordingly' (*Daily Telegraph*, 26 January 1971). Throughout, further evidence was provided of the insidious magnetic hold that Manson exercised over his followers. He appeared in court with an 'X' cut into his forehead and later with a shaved head declaring that he was the devil. The three women did the same. They also played up for the news media in what they said, how they dressed and how they behaved, showing no signs of remorse during proceedings. This included jeering at the relatives of the victims. Outside the courthouse, the cohesive loyalty of the Manson family was demonstrated by followers conducting a 24-hour-a-day vigil, condemning the 'second crucifixion of Christ,' passing on messages from 'Charlie' and warning of revenge (Bugliosi and Gentry, 1974: 443).

On 29 March 1971 Charlie Manson, the master manipulator, and his co-defendants were sentenced to death, but those sentences switched to life imprisonment after California temporarily banned the death penalty in 1972. Later that year another family member, Charles 'Tex' Watson, was convicted of the Tate-La Bianca murders, and Manson was also convicted of the murders of Gary Hinman, a family member, and Donald Shea, a Hollywood stunt man who was killed at Spahn Movie Ranch in late August of 1969. After his conviction Manson released a defiant address to the nation:

> Mr and Mrs America – you are wrong. I am not the King of the Jews nor am I a hippie cult leader. I am what you have made of me and the mad dog devil killer fiend leper is a reflection of your society … Whatever the outcome of this madness that you call a fair trial or Christian justice, you can know this: in my mind's eye my thoughts light fires in your cities.
>
> (Bugliosi and Gentry, 1974: 539)

## WHAT IS THE FUTURE OF DOOMSDAY CULTS?

Charlie Manson's doomsday cult continues to have a profound impact on the American psyche, intensely evocative of a specific time and place. Manson, the dangerously charismatic cult leader, 'Mansonism' and the homicidal actions of the 'Mansonites' have been written into popular culture and the social history of the cultic moment of the late 1960s and early 1970s (Riley, 2019). As a result, Manson achieved the celebrity status that he had always craved.

The trial and the commentary surrounding it popularised the term 'cult,' publicised the dangers of cults and galvanised an emergent anti-cult movement. This was the first public airing of debates about brainwashing, mind control, programming, charismatic pathology, cultish language and followership issues that would become central to cult studies. Discussion continues to focus on how a group of middle-class young women could be moulded by 'a half-assed nothing who hardly knew how to read or write' (Emmons, 2019: 222) into 'killer zombies' who believed they were triggering '*Helter Skelter.*'

> The most fascinating part of the Manson story has always been the girls …. The ones willing and vulnerable enough to be gathered. Who wanted a community to belong to…They believed. They belonged.
>
> (Beck, 2016; see also Gilbert, 2017)

What was truly shocking looking at the photographs and news footage was that these young women looked exactly like suburbia's daughters, granddaughters, sisters, girlfriends, babysitters and neighbours (Meredith, 2018).

Conspiratorial argument also persists about:

- the real motivations for the Tate-LaBianca killings;
- how many more murders the Manson family was responsible for before and after the arrests;
- the influence of California's satanic cultic milieu on Manson's apocalyptic thinking;
- the true nature of Manson's relationship with the Los Angeles' music establishment.

(Sanders, 1971; Capote, 1980;; Guinn, 2013; Dyrendal et al., 2015; Melnick, 2018; Emmons, 2019; O'Neill, 2019)

The murderous doomsday cult was appropriated politically. There was incredulity on the political right that Manson had not only escaped the death penalty but 'Mansonmania' was enabling him to achieve folk hero status. The fear was that he would be able to exert control over the remnants of the family, attract new 'Mansonites' and continue to decide who had the right to live and who did not (Adams, 1972). In August 1971 members of the Manson family were involved in a gun battle with police in Los Angeles and in 1975 Lynette 'Squeaky' Fromme, one of Manson's most ardent followers, attempted to assassinate President Gerald Ford. Unrepentant, she served 34 years in prison (Fromme, 2022).

Until his death, Manson, America's most notorious criminal, received the largest amount of fan mail in the history of the US prison system with numerous offers of marriage. The Tate family and their supporters became an important part of the emergent victims' rights movement in the US, establishing the Doris Tate Crime Victims' Bureau. It tracked the prison careers of Manson, Watson, Atkins, Kasabian, Krenwinkel and Van Houten and mobilised public opposition to every attempt made by them to obtain parole (Statman and Tate, 2021).

Initially, for sections of the radical left, Manson was a larger-than-life 'anti-hero' who was undermining the dominant value system. Some characterised him as a 'political prisoner' who had been framed by the establishment to discredit the hippy movement

(O'Neill, 2019). Throughout his trial and time in prison Manson insisted that he had never killed anyone or ordered others to do so. On the contrary, he stressed that he had tried to rein in his followers' murderous inclinations. Other 'Mansonites,' such as the Weather Underground, applauded the 'hippy terrorist' for declaring war on rich, privileged 'La La Land' 'piggies' who deserved to die (Jacobs, 1997). The front page of *Life* magazine for 19 December 1969 was given over to a 'wild eyed' photograph of 'cult leader' Manson with the headline 'The Love and Terror Cult.' *Rolling Stone* also ran features on 'the family' with a Christ-like photograph of Manson, describing him as 'the Most Dangerous Man Alive' and 'the face-of-evil superstar symbol, second only to Hitler.' Jerry Rubin, who visited Manson in prison, exclaimed: 'I fell in love with Charlie Manson the first time I saw his cherub face and sparkling eyes on TV… His words and courage inspired us' (Bugliosi and Gentry 1974: 286).

For the liberal left, Manson, 'the mutant hippy,' was to blame for turning the countercultural dream represented by the 'Summer of Love' and Woodstock into a nightmare (Lachman, 2001; Donaghey, 2019). Joan Didion (1979: 47) noted; 'Many people I know in Los Angeles believe that the '60s ended abruptly on August 9, 1969 at the exact moment when word of the murders on Cielo Drive travelled like brushfire through the community.' The ramifications for well-established hippy communes and new religious movements were serious as they were now re-conceptualised by American society as dangerous cults. Manson, 'the deranged racist,' was also viewed as part of the violent backlash against the civil rights movement and a touchstone for white supremacist cults who were preparing for an inevitable race war. This was seemingly confirmed when he reworked the X on his forehead into a swastika in order to identify himself with the Aryan Brotherhood (Grann, 2004). And then there was Manson 'the misogynist.' Gore Vidal (1971) formulated a prototype male called 'M3,' an equation for Henry Miller+Norman Mailer+Charlie Manson, exemplars of the sort of man who thinks that women are 'at best, breeders of sons; at worst, objects to be poked, humiliated, killed.'

Unsurprisingly, America's celebrity culture also appropriated the 'Manson family.' Manson's name became synonymous with the Beatles' 'Helter Skelter', Sharon Tate, Roman Polanski, the Beach Boys, the fabled Californian 'summer of love,' Altamont and the moon landing. After his conviction, Manson released more compilations of his songs, including *Live at San Quentin*, and in the early 1970s eight of the remaining family recorded as the 'Manson Family Singers.' In contemporary pop music he has featured in the recordings of underground groups such as Throbbing Gristle, Psychic TV, Black Flag and Sonic Youth. There have been cover versions of Manson's own songs by Nine Inch Nails, Marilyn Manson (his persona 'a commentary on the creation of celebrity') and Guns 'n' Roses. The rock group Kasabian is named after family member Linda Kasabian, who later went on to testify against Manson at his trial.

During the 1980s, Manson gave four interviews to the mainstream media which once more re-imprinted his 'evil incarnate' cult leader persona into public consciousness. There are Manson family films, docudramas and documentaries, as well as a play, a musical, an opera and Manson-esque novels (Cooper, 2018: Melnick, 2018). An upsurge in interest followed the 2019 release of four films featuring the Manson family, including Quentin Tarantino's *Once Upon a Time in Hollywood*.

Charlie Manson has appeared in the US cartoon series *Family Guy* and *The Simpsons* and on a bewildering array of T-shirts, badges and websites which carry clips of his interviews and parole appearances. His own website at one time promoted the idea of Manson as an eco warrior. When Manson died in 2017 he might have been gratified to know that obituaries were carried in major news outlets confirming him as the cult leader who 'killed the 1960s.' More recently, the mythology of the Manson family has been revamped due to the true crime podcast and broadcast boom, most notably *Charles Manson's Hollywood* and *How to become a Cult Leader*.

The 'Mansonites' may have failed to ignite an apocalyptic race war or be 'bigger than the Beatles' but through the Tate-LaBianca killing spree and the subsequent trial they achieved cult mythos status and in fully intermediatised form endure as a source of endless cultural fascination. The Manson family provides the template for any doomsday cult seeking, through superconductive acts of spectacular violence, to capture the public imagination and/or any prospective apocalyptic guru harbouring ambitions to become immortalised as a counter cultural icon.

## REFERENCES

Adams, V. (1972). Psychology of murder. *Time*, 24 April.
Atkins, S. (2005). *Child of Satan, child of God*. Dorenay's Publishing.
Barker, E. (1989). *New religious movements: a practical introduction*. Home Office.
Beam, M. (1964). *Cults of America*. MacFadden-Bartell Corporation.
Beck, J. (2016). Charles Manson, the girls, and the banality of desire. *The Atlantic*, 26 July.
Bohm, J. and Alison, L. (2001). An exploratory study in methods of distinguishing destructive cults. *Psychology, Crime and Law*, 7, 131–165.
Bugliosi, V. and Gentry, C. (1974). *Helter skelter: the true story of the Manson murders*. Arrow Books.
Capote, T. (1980). *Music for chameleons*. Penguin.
Conway, F. and Siegelman, J. (2005). *Snapping: America's epidemic of sudden personality change*. Still Point Press.
Cooper, I. (2018). *The Manson family on film and television*. McFarland and Co.
Didion, Joan (1979). *The white album*. Simon & Schuster.
Donaghey, R. (2019). How Charles Manson put an end to the hippie movement. *VICE*, 7 June.
Dyrendal, A., Lewis, J.R. and Petersen, J. (2015). *Invention of Satanism*. Oxford University Press.
Eco, U., Gould, S.J., Carriere, J.C and Delumeau, J. (1999). *Conversations about the end of time*. Penguin.
Emmons, N. (2019). *Manson in his own words*. Grove Press.
Faith, K. (2001). *The long prison journey of Lesley Van Houten*. Northeastern Press.
Felton, D. and Dalton, D. (1970). Charles Manson: the incredible story of the most dangerous man alive. *Rolling Stone*, 25 June 1970 (available at: http://www.rollingstone.com/culture/news/charles-manson-the-incredible-story-of-the-most-dangerousman-alive-19700625).
Festinger, L., Riecken, H.W and Schachter, S. (2009). *When prophecy fails*. Martino Publishing.
Folk, Z. (2023) Elon Musk boasts cyber truck is 'apocalypse proof' at live deliver event. *Forbes*, 30 November.
Fromme, L. (2022). *Reflexion*. Peasenhal Press.
Frykholm, A. (2004). *Rapture culture: left behind in evangelical America*. Oxford University Press.
Gilbert, S. (2017). The real cult of Charles Manson. *The Atlantic*, 20 November.
Grann, D. (2004). The brand. *New Yorker*, 16 February.
Guinn, J. (2013). *Manson: the life and times of Charles Manson*. Simon and Schuster.
Hall, J.R., Schuyler, P.D. and Trinh, S. (2000). *Apocalypse observed: religious movements and violence in North America*. Routledge.

Hedegaard, E. (2013). Charles Manson today: the final confessions of a psychopath. *Rolling Stone*, 5 December.
Jacobs, R. (1997). *The way the wind blew: a history of the Weather Underground*. Verso.
Kabel, A. and Chmidling, C. (2014). Disaster prepper: health, identity, and American survivalist culture. *Human Organization*, 73(3), 258–266.
Kaplan, D.E. and Marshall, A. (1996). *The cult at the end of the world*. Crown Publishers.
Lachman, G. (2001). *Turn off your mind: the mystic sixties and the dark side of the age of Aquarius*. The Disinformation Company.
La Ganga, M.L. and Himmelsbach-Weinstein, E. (2019). Charles Manson's murderous imprint on L.A. endures as other killers have come and gone. *Los Angeles Times*, 28 July.
Lake, D. (2018). *Member of the family: Manson, murder and me*. Harper Element.
Leary, T. (1999). *Turn on, tune in, drop out*. Ronin Books.
*Life* (2019). *Manson*. Meredith Corporation.
Lifton, R.J. (1961). *Thought reform and the psychology of totalism*. W.W. Norton.
Lifton, R.J. (1999). *Destroying the world to save it*. Henry Holt and Co.
Lifton, R.J. (2019). *Losing reality*. The New Press.
Lofland, J. (1966). *Doomsday cults: a study of conversion, proselytization and maintenance of faith*. Prentice Hall.
Melnick, J. (2018). *Creepy crawling: Charles Manson and the many lives of America's most infamous family*. Arcade Publishing.
Meredith, N. (2018). *The Manson girls and me*. Citadel Press.
Mills, M.F. (2019). Preparing for the unknown ... unknowns: 'doomsday' prepping and disaster risk anxiety in the United States. *Journal of Risk Research*, 22 (10), 1267–1279.
Montell, A. (2021). *Cultish: the language of fanaticism*. HarperCollins.
Nielsen, D.A. (1984). Charles Manson's family of love: a case study of anomism, puerilism and transmoral consciousness in civilizational perspective. *Sociology of Religion*, 45(4), 315–337.
O'Leary, S.D. (1998). *Arguing the apocalypse: a theory of millennial rhetoric*. Oxford University Press.
O'Neill, T. (2019). *Chaos: the truth behind the Manson murders*. Penguin Books.
Pagels, E. (2012). *Revelations: visions, prophesy and politics in the Book of Revelation*. Penguin.
Riley, J. (2019). *The bad trip: dark omens, new worlds and the end of the sixties*. Icon Books.
Roberts, S.V. (1969). All the twists are bizarre in the Tate case. *New York Times*, 7 December, E4).
Rushkoff, D. (2022). *Survival of the richest: escape fantasies of the tech billionaires*. Scribe.

Sanders, E. (1971). *The family: the story of Charles Manson's dune buggy attack battalion*. E.P. Dutton.

Sanders, E. (2019). Why pop culture still can't get enough of Charles Manson. *New York Times*, 24 July.

Statman, A. and Tate, B. (2021). *Restless souls: the Sharon Tate family account of stardom, the Manson murders, and a crusade for justice*. HarperCollins.

Sutton, M.A. (2014). *American apocalypse: a history of modern evangelicalism*. Harvard University Press.

Thompson, D. (1999). *The end of time*. Vintage.

Thunberg, G. (ed.) (2022). *The climate book*. Penguin.

Vidal, G. (1971). In another country. *New York Review of Books*, 22 July.

Watson, C. (2019). *Cease to exist: a firsthand account of indoctrination into the Manson family*.

Wells, S. (2009). *Charles Manson: coming down fast*. Hodder and Stoughton.

Wiehl, L. (2018). *Hunting Charles Manson*. Nelson Books.

# CELEBRITY CULTS
## YE (KANYE WEST)

## WHAT IS A CELEBRITY CULT?

A celebrity cult is a social multitude with potent affective bonds to an external figure of presence in the market for attention. There are three types of celebrity. *Ascribed Celebrities* possess renown by reason of heredity or the titular position that they occupy, via tradition or enfranchisement. Examples include kings, queens, emperors, empresses, sultans, popes, presidents and prime ministers. *Achieved Celebrities* acquire renown by virtue of their personal talents, skills and accomplishments. They include sports stars, film stars, pop idols, fashion icons and business titans. *Celetoids* possess fame via media saturation. Examples include reality TV stars, figures of notoriety and ordinary citizens who are momentarily recognised for civic merit, charitable acts, heroism or nefarious deeds. Hence, there are three categories of celebrity cults: Ascribed, Achieved, Celetoid. Unquestionably, followers are energised by shared beliefs, opinions, wants and prejudices independent of celebrity presence. Nevertheless, withal, the focus is upon the celebrity. The intensity and duration of celebrity cults attached to a celebrity category varies. This is because, at the level of perceived meaning, there are many fibres of affective alignment. They include image, values, beliefs, feelings.

A helpful way to simplify this is to propose that the nucleus of the relationship between a cult and a celebrity is *unpunctuated consciousness*. That is, the conviction of cult members that they and celebrities are intimately on the same wavelength. In sociology the concept of charisma was introduced by Max Weber to refer to a leader who is perceived as having 'supernatural' or at least 'exceptional' powers (Weber 1978). The concept is germane to the subject of celebrity. In Weber's sociology the concept meant leaders that produce catalytic, transformative society-wide change. Nowadays, this is so rare that most sociologists treat fully developed charismatic authority as a thing of the past. However, there is backing for the notion that commercialised, packaged forms of charisma persist in the celebration of people who are held to be of noteworthiness. Borrowing and repurposing the concept of 'derived charisma' from Bryan Wilson, it might reasonably be proposed that elements of charisma clearly survive in celebrity cults (Wilson, 1975: 116–119). Thus, achieved and celetoid cults adhere to close cognitive and emotional sympathies invested in external figures of perceived affirmative presence. Indeed, the concept of unpunctuated consciousness denotes not only recognition of similarity between beholders and external celebrity presence, but also the idea that celebrities are extraordinary expressions of universal form.

In the case of ascribed cults the situation is somewhat different. Here affective bonding is ultimately based upon the esteemed, official *position* that a celebrity occupies in the traditional (often portrayed as 'immemorial') social hierarchy. Nevertheless, unpunctuated consciousness remains relevant since cult membership is mobilised and solidifies around the symbolic compulsion to honour titular rank that symbolises sublime, epic gravity, e.g. 'the nation,' 'the people,' 'the denomination,' 'divine historical precedent,' etc. Under unpunctuated consciousness the connection between the celebrity and the cult is experienced as glaringly obvious and irrefutable. Therefore, no objective proof is required. The current of inner life is perceived to resonate so closely with celebrity presence that the relationship between the two is palpably experienced as one of confirmation. In terms of the social mechanics of the reaction, the external celebrity object is perceived to crystallise the thoughts, feelings and taste predilections that run through the minds of cult members. Needless to say, cult responses are conditioned by relations of gender, class, age, race, ethnicity and cognate social variables. However, the emotional charge of membership is too all-encompassing for an explanation that relies solely upon a framework of cultural relativism. As the term 'unpunctuated consciousness' implies, the logistics of cult membership exceed empirical social variables. They pertain to questions of *interiority*, i.e. *pre-social* intuitions and intimations concerning awareness of being, belonging and direction that elevated figures of noteworthy, external presence appear to verify. Celebrity cult members relate to celebrities as more acute versions of what is gleaned intuitively of their inner selves. Intuition and intimation are therefore important methodological routes of cult consciousness. As will be apparent presently, both have been neglected by the mainstream of cult studies which limits valid knowledge to quantifiable, empirically accessible data. Citing intuition and intimation as intrinsic to cult consciousness therefore runs against the grain. However, the position taken here is that, on theoretical and methodological grounds, accurate analysis cannot do without them.

The affirmative relationship between a celebrity cult and a celebrity is signalled visually. *Inter alia,* meaningful identification is relayed by wardrobe choice, cosmetics, grooming, vocabulary, declared outlook, posture, bearing and bodily insignia (such as piercings and tattoos). The *attention capital* of celebrity is something that the celebrity cult exchanges in order to register preferred forms of social belonging and to exercise social impact (Franck, 2019). At the subjective level, the main reason for this is that investing in the attention capital of celebrities translates into profile upgrade in life with others. A whole branch of celebrity studies has become established that takes as its main academic preoccupation investigating the designs, transactions and consequences of celebrity *persona* (Marshall, Moore and Barbour, 2015; Marshall, 2016). Analytically, this assists in elucidating how celebrity presence supports inter-subjective meaning in the cult multitude and how it is labelled by others.

Celebrity cults are not just qualitative congeries in which members share meanings and outlooks. They are also economic assets. From the standpoint of economics, attention capital is a resource to enhance price and utility. The value of attention capital is a function of celebrity elevation and presence. Both determine economic margin. They are co-dependent with the quantification of social impact. Quantification is measured by a variety of metrics, including attendance data, circulation figures, box office returns, media profile and endorsement dividend (the value generated by the alignment between a celebrity and an independent retail brand). The principal standard of celebrity value is face and name recognition. Instant recognition is an economic resource that can be readily converted into financial yield. Celebrity cults are therefore concrete resources for economic accumulation. Instant name and face recognition is compatible with a variety of income bearing outputs. Celebrity endorsements are an obvious example. By matching celebrity glamour at the point of sale with an independent commodity brand, market advantage may be acquired. Celebrity endorsement for retail commodities such as sunglasses, automobiles, trainers, perfumes, luxury attire, etc., has a general proven economic track record of augmenting marginal utility. In a digitally connected world, trading instant recognition as intellectual property has important income stream and asset value outcomes. The three main components of intellectual property are: (1) *copyright*: the exclusive right to reproduce, publish and communicate a legally protected item to the public; (2) *trade-mark*: an insignia attached to a particular good or service; and (3) *franchise*: legally binding arrangements that regulate the packaging and distribution of a celebrity image over defined platforms and territories. Celebrity presence over celebrity cults can therefore be thought of as *rental value*. That is, various mechanisms of intellectual property investment may be allocated to transfer the quantitively measurable cult attachment of a celebrity presence to separate, remote areas of the market. In this way, rental purchase relays value to copyrighted, trademarked and franchised goods to enhance the cultic appeal and sale of commodities (King, 2010).

The strong connections between celebrity presence and economic value have driven some critics to deplore modern celebrity culture as a culture of empty renown. For example, Daniel Boorstin analyses celebrity as mostly a contrived construct that follows a technocratic blueprint to maximise economic return (Boorstin, 1962). The engrossing captivation here is with the inauthenticity of celebrity and what is seen as its sordid effects upon civilisation. The days when celebrity signified nobility, improvement and *dignitas* have long gone. For Boorstin, modern celebrity culture revolves around consumption and accumulation. In the same vein, Postman dwells upon what he takes to be its degrading effect in encouraging 'anti-communication, featuring a type of discourse that abandons logic, reason, sequence, and rules of contradiction' (Postman,

1987: 105). The primary functions of celebrity today are to amuse and entertain, not to inform and educate. Therefore, Boorstin and Postman are as one in abhorring modern celebrity culture for debasing civil society. Writing in a different (neo-Marxist) tradition, Adorno reaches broadly the same conclusion. In his view celebrity culture plays an immense confidence trick on beholders:

> The ideological function of (celebrity) biographies is to demonstrate to people through some kind of models that something like a life, possessed of all the emphatic categories of life still exists and, indeed, precisely in an empirical context which those who have no more life can reclaim for themselves.
> (Adorno, in Lowenthal, 1989: 141–142)

All of these critics equate celebrity with deception. Further, they suggest that celebrity cults elicit consciousness of integration and purpose that is based in mystification.

While the culture of empty renown position remains highly influential it has generated an academic critical reaction. For example, Gamson refers to celebrity culture as an assembly line of greatness' (Gamson, 2001: 259). However, he refuses to stop there. Instead, he gives due to the capacity of audiences to read celebrity texts in their own language and to game the received, ideological images of emphatic life (Gamson, 1994: 173). Other critics point to the emergence and vitality of gossip sites, fan sites and blog platforms that elaborate and challenge the circulation of managed outputs of elevation and presence (Marwick and boyd, 2011: 139). A closed reading of celebrity and celebrity cults that pairs them exclusively with technocratic, managed outputs is thus opposed.

## WHY DO CELEBRITY CULTS EMERGE?

Academic enquiry into celebrities and celebrity cults is generally conducted via an analytic framework that focuses upon the interchange between three empirically distinct and accessible agents: *celebrities*, *media* and *publics* (Marcus, 2019). Celebrities are individuals that possess noteworthy presence via stakeholder (celebrity industry) aid. The *media* refers to the ensemble of different institutions of mass communication that have a pronounced influence upon the repertoire and accumulation of celebrity representations. *Publics* refers to differentiated forms and mediums of consumption, exchange and transaction in the market of representation and attention. Celebrity cults are differentiated forms and mediums situated within publics. Attention capital is dependent upon the combined and uneven development of relations between the three agents. The agents are well established and durable. The balance of power between them is not. There are circumstances where the reaction of publics can neutralise and overthrow the strategies of managed outputs sought by stakeholders and the media. Be that as it may, historically, stakeholder and media influence has repeatedly exerted disproportionate influence upon elevation and presence. The role of the media in communicating celebrity and summoning-up celebrity cults is designated as paramount. In the words of Driessens, celebrities are products of 'accumulated media visibility' (Driessens, 2014: 115). Upon this basis he invites readers to investigate celebrities as the result of 'recurring media representations' (Driessens, 2014: 115). Significantly, media planning is theorised as preceding the wants, needs and desires of celebrity cults. As such, the research task is self-evident. It consists in scaling and quantifying the effects of media output upon social consciousness. By addressing the variable depth and range of media flows, the magnitude and dynamics of celebrity presence in celebrity cults will inevitably be revealed.

Additionally, this analytic framework helps to periodise celebrity. Acclaim and renown were of course, preoccupations of past societies. For example, both Greece and Rome understood them to derive from noble deeds and extraordinary personalities. In each social order this was insufficient to confer fame. The favour of the gods was also required (Cicero, 1950). The hand of religion was far more significant in popular conceptions of fame and acclaim than it is nowadays. The influence of the gods upon human affairs was perceived as indivisible. Crucially, it was also granted to be mysterious and ineffable. In these societies responsibility for accountability with respect to acclaim and renown was primarily a matter for oral culture, especially public oratory. As such, the curators of fame were overwhelmingly the noble and patrician strata that occupied the central public offices of power and could read and write. Acclaim and fame in ancient society obeyed different logistics, consisted of a contrasting affective intensity and operated with a mode of communication that curtailed the evolution of associated cults.

The age of celebrity depended upon three prerequisites: the rise of the media and print culture; the growth of literacy; the concentration of urban populations; and the flourishing of democracy. The preconditions that supported a durable interchange between agents of celebrity, media and publics were not *in situ* until the middle of the eighteenth century (Lilti, 2017: 82–100). Consecutively changes in the perception of elevation and the categorisation of public noteworthy presence became visible. However, these transpositions are not now allied cognitively with a gift of the gods. Nor are they conceived as independent and self-perpetuating. Rather, they are conceptualised as the consequences of technology. Celebrity is born when technology makes mass communications possible. In the trinity of celebrities, media and publics, the role usually attributed to the media in analysis is paramount. *In fine*, mass media is assigned the power to create the cult of personality (Marcus, 2019: 76). Marcus's case studies of the cults affixed to the nineteenth-century celebrities Sarah Bernhardt and Oscar Wilde gives full due to the effect of newspapers, periodicals, photography and mass-produced souvenirs in stimulating and solidifying cult integration.

In the mainstream then, analysis is therefore predisposed to adopt a supply-side approach to celebrity and celebrity cults. Attention capital is explored as the managed outcome of the combined strategic investment of stakeholders in celebrity presence (the celebrity Industry) and the media (the main path dependent influence on social consciousness of celebrity). The question of celebrity demand is treated as a dependent variable of stakeholder-media capitalisation. Demand-side enquiries to de-capitalise the meaning of celebrity, by investigating formative beholder wants, beliefs, needs and desires that are *anterior* to elevation and presence, either fall by the wayside, or are discounted *tout court*.

## HOW ARE CELEBRITY CULTS ESTABLISHED AND MAINTAINED?

Celebrity cultures are ubiquitous. Examples can be drawn from any number of sectors including sport, theatre, television, film, literature, science and politics. The case study selected here is

Kanye West. The motivation for focusing on West is partly the sheer quantitative scale of his popularity. In September 2023 his Twitter account listed 31.7 million followers. Beyond doubt, West possesses instant global name and face recognition. It might even be ventured that he is part of the select higher echelon in celebrity culture, namely a celebrity icon, i.e. an individual that sums up the age. He is a *bona fide* achieved celebrity. The cult attached to him respects him as a role model of success and upward mobility.

West was born in Atlanta and raised in Chicago. His background was black bourgeois. His mother was a professor and Chair of the Department of English, Communications and Media at Chicago State University, and his father was a photo-journalist (and former Black Panther). His family of origin was politicised around the racial divide in America. This is what one would expect for someone who initially gained celebrity as a rap producer, composer and performer. Significantly, whereas the majority of rap/hip hop celebrities emerge from the precariat, West came from a relatively privileged, cosmopolitan, bookish background. He enrolled to study English at Chicago State University but dropped out to pursue a musical career.

His entry point into celebrity culture was as a rap technocrat. He worked as a producer for rap artists such as Jay Z, Freeway and Talib Kwell. As a technical designer for performers, he would have been conscious of the wants, needs and desires of the target audience and the communication power of the media. His celebrity elevation and presence accelerated and magnified after he transitioned to become a performer. His debut studio album, *The College Dropout*, was released in 2004. It was an instant success. It received Album of the Year and Best Rap Album awards at the 2005 Grammy ceremony. In 2020 the Recording Industry Association of America certified its sales as four times platinum. Rap/Hip Hop is the soundtrack of the twenty-first century. West has been at the vanguard for over 20 years. From the beginning, a large and enduring feature of his appeal has been asymmetry. He is on the oppressed side of the colour line, but his family was middle class, and he grew up critical of the Civil Rights settlement. He was a rap technocrat before he released his own rap compositions. In addition, when all is said and done, he does not fit the gangsta rap stereotype. Granted, the themes covered in *The College Dropout* addressed stock rap terrain e.g. racism, family, sexuality, prejudice, religion, consumerism and justice. But West's treatment is more reflexive and analytic. Crucially, it is also far more entrepreneurial. He related to popular culture not only in artistic terms but as a Strategic Investment Vehicle (SIV). From the start, he incorporated his perception of unmet audience status, mobility and purchasing wants and needs into his commercial output. One sign of this is that he quickly spun his rap music presence into 'bespoke aggregation' (Rojek, 2011: 163–165). That is, the exploitation and development of celebrity status in one sector of the economy, via trade-marking franchise agreements, copyright and direct investment, into multiple sectors. West advanced his business interests on at least four fronts: music, fashion, creative content management and politics. In doing so he created an all-encompassing narrative of lifestyle preference. The celebrity cults that emerged revered West as a figure to emulate. This favoured status was reinforced by his material success. His 'Yeezy' fashion line, that collaborated with Nike, Adidas, Louis Vuitton, Balenciaga and Gap, gained significant market share. His DONDA company trades in creative content. It is a vehicle for imposing an aesthetic thumbprint upon hip hop/rap culture via graphic design, sport wellness and film production. It has announced plans to move into the high-tech sector with lines in surround-sound systems, audio speakers, computers, tablets and smartwatches (2022). The essence of cult integration is identification and commitment. West's lifestyle companies make consumption of the commodities that they produce the insignia of these cult characteristics.

In 2022 their aggregate trading position was seriously impaired by a series of damaging controversies surrounding West's public behaviour. He wore a 'White Lives Matter' T shirt at the Paris Fashion Week; in an appearance on the conspiracy theorist Alex Jones' TV show, with the white nationalist commentator Nick Fuentes, he made apologist remarks about aspects of Hitler's leadership; and his Twitter and Instagram accounts were temporarily suspended for tweeting anti-Semitic material (Monk-Payton, 2023: 21). West has a long history of making contentious remarks in public. In 2005 during a televised post-Katrina recovery event, 'A Concert for Hurricane Relief,' he declared that 'George Bush [the president] doesn't care about black people' (George, 2016: 18). The 2022 controversies damaged West's bespoke aggregation trading position. Following his anti-Semitic outbursts, franchise partnerships with Adidas, Balenciaga and Gap were terminated. TJ Max and Foot Locker announced plans to de-stock 'Yeezy' merchandise. MRC Entertainment and Vogue boycotted commercial business with West. West legally changed his name to Ye in 2021. He had announced his intention to do so in 2018. This was concomitant with his born-again Christian evangelicalism. In a reported radio interview, he explained: 'I believe "ye" is the most commonly used word in the Bible, and in the Bible means you. So I'm you, I'm us, it's us. "Ye" is just a reflection of our good, our bad, our confused everything' (*Guardian*, 19 October 2021). The Christian commitment also carries the meaning of spiritual salvation and leaving the material world behind.

Ye's self-declared wish to automatically represent 'our confused everything' is revealing. His default public manner is to behave as if he has impunity. The threefold game plan is to express cult power, to confound expectations and to generate publicity. The logic is straightforward. By generating media attention, profile is raised and market noteworthiness is enhanced. This was to the fore in Ye's infamous presidential campaigns in 2020 and 2024. With mediocre projected polling support, nonetheless, Ye campaigned in 2020 on a scripture-based independent ticket of environmentalism, investment in creative culture, reform of the justice system, economic protectionism, household debt and student loan reduction, and increased spending on defence. The bid floundered upon faulty ballot provision (he met candidacy registration requirements in only 12 states), desultory electioneering and confused messaging. In 2022 he announced his intention to run in the 2024 campaign. There are reasonable grounds for doubting the integrity of the pledge. Electioneering was underwhelming. Press statements took the place of debate/questioning. Campaign stumping was minimal. Ye was not listed as one of the 17 declared candidates published by the *New York Times* in August 2023 (Gomez and Astor, 2023).

Ye's audacity reveals something vital about his iconic status. *Displacement* rather than placement is the key to his iconic position.

His upbringing coincided with 'the fault line that simultaneously joined and separated the Civil Rights and Black Power movements' (Ciccarello-Maher, 2009: 385). Several commentators have observed that 'double consciousness' is indispensable for understanding Ye's public behaviour (Ciccarello-Maher, 2009; Richardson, 2011: 102). The term was coined by Du Bois to refer to the state of mind of the racially oppressed which recognises 'two warring ideals in one dark body,' i.e. the definition of themselves imposed upon them by the racially dominant strata and their self-image formed and sustained via *habitus* and community aspiration (Du Bois, 1903: 38). Ye belongs to the post-double consciousness generation of the American colour line. That is, he rejects the stereotypical identity imposed upon him by racially dominant strata, while at the same time deploring the settlement achieved by the African-American vanguard in the Civil Rights trauma. This is consistent with his readiness to overturn cultural assumptions. Sporting a MAGA cap and endorsing the Trump presidency; wearing a 'White Lives Matter' T shirt; expressing sympathies with aspects of Hitler's leadership; making anti-Semitic comments, can all be read as acts of *bricolage* that have the same clandestine end in view: 'the marketization of audacity' (Lofton, 2021: 96–97; Monk-Payton, 2023: 21). Whether Ye believes in the controversial things he says and does is irrelevant. The payload is that he is making transparent what large sections of society conceal. His audacity is therefore recognised as a form of integrity. This carries over into the commodity range offered to consumers in Ye's brand. If one buys Yeezy Boost 350 sneakers (that currently retail for £269.23 in the UK) one gets an entry card to a cult figure who is fearless in calling out the hypocrisy of mass culture. The proof of the pudding is in the eating.

## WHAT IS THE FUTURE OF CELEBRITY CULTS?

Ye's marketisation of audacity resonates with widespread sentiments of cultural, political and economic displacement. The modernisation project of post-war reconstruction was based upon principles of differentiation. The affluent society would abolish want and poverty. Civil inclusion and welfare rights would extend to all.

Reason and rationality would replace religion and superstition. Upward mobility would be incorporated into the newly emerging civic structure. Wealth would be reallocated on the principle of distributive justice. Above all, modernisation would introduce an evidence-based framework for recognising rights and determining resource allocation. The great prize for all of this was that consensus would inevitably replace division. Modernisation is now widely judged to be a defective project (Calhoun, Gaonkar and Taylor, 2022). Leaving aside the question of its faults, among its virtues was predicted to be rendering charisma obsolescent. 'The likelihood,' wrote Wilson in law-like terms, 'of a socially significant manifestation of charisma diminishes with technical advance' (Wilson, 1975: 104). In our own time, the scale of the cultic moment and the proliferation of celebrity cults disproves this proposition. Celebrity cults exploit and develop forms of diverted charisma to accumulate followers and build attention capital. Technical advance has been appropriated by celebrities and the media to raise elevation and concentrate presence in public consciousness. Modernisation has not inexorably built consensus. Rather, the present age is widely seen as defined by social malaise in which division, indignation and uncertainty prevail.

Ye was born in 1977. This was a juncture when the experience of differentiation began to be challenged by de-differentiation. The oil crisis punctured the confidence of affluent society in perpetual material progress. The catastrophic adventurism of America in the Vietnam war and the carpet bombing of Cambodia, toxified belief in the sovereignty of evidence-based, rational state decision-making. Growing anxieties about environmental decay, urban blight, male power, institutional racism, inadequate public services, notably education and welfare and family violence, were among other things the seed beds of hip hop/rap culture. Rap employs quotidian vocabularies and narratives to communicate individual, subaltern positions and predicaments into wider communities of meaning, belonging and power (Pope, 2020: 4). It utilises selective manipulation of technology combined with rhythmic chanting and street speech to explore issues of poverty, authority, chaos, violence and resistance. Outwardly, it is concerned with giving power to the powerless. But its moral compass suggests that deeply rooted structures of hypocrisy, injustice and elite domination are experienced fatalistically as invincible. Seen in this light it is an error to fall into the common media presentation of Ye's public conduct as seizing upon expediency without observing oversight. His grandiose disruption of the authority of any sign to define and fix meaning, be it Civil Rights victories, abhorrence of Hitler, prohibition of anti-Semitic remarks, is deliberate. It is meant to have a legacy. For him, activism means subverting conventional perspectives and unexamined convictions in order to truly free publics from the crust of subjugation. The goal is not so much to expose the hidden meaning of authority and replace it with an untainted alternative. Rather, it is to question *all* forms of authority on the grounds that any meaning is contingent, inherently ambivalent and therefore temporary.

The marketisation of audacity as the cement for cult formation is only one path taken in the cultic moment. Other celebrity cults offer glamour, integrity and salvation. Common to all is fidelity to transcendence. Celebrity cults are a provocation to normative order because they provide intimations of complete, fulfilled, necessary, consummate states of being. Celebrities that present themselves as displaced from normative order are a staging post for those who feel under-estimated, side-lined, damaged or belittled. The corollary of all of this is that normative order is itself insufficient and must be surpassed. The degree to which this is possible in late capitalist societies is an open question. To Adorno's point, celebrities supply public images of the whole life and encourage beholder emulation in structural conditions of economic inequality and political manipulation that align to compromise the realistic possibility of meaningful wider change. It is fair to propose that gaming and redefining received messaging are compatible with celebrity culture managed outputs (Gamson, 1994; Marwick and boyd, 2011). The churn turns on the issue of degree. How far do gaming and redefinition challenge an entrenched celebrity culture in which the celebrity industry and the media normatively have disproportionate power over publics?

This is an issue that has outlasted the argument made in the culture of empty renown tradition that celebrity culture is malign and must be dismantled (Boorstin, 1962; Postman, 1987). Some types of celebrity and associated celebrity cults are positive influences in society. They provide companionship, inspiration and purpose to millions of people who find life beyond isolating and unfulfilling. There is no turning back the clock on celebrity culture. What is necessary is to devise effective ways of precisely developing an inventory of its effects and regulating output accordingly.

## REFERENCES

Boorstin, D. (1962). *The image*. Penguin.

Calhoun, C., Gaonkar, D.P. and Taylor, C. (2022). *Degenerations of democracy*. Harvard University Press.

Ciccarello-Maher, G. (2009). A critique of Du Bosian reason: Kanye West and the fruitfulness of double-consciousness. *Journal of Black Studies*, 39(3), 371–491.

Cicero, M.T. (1950). *Brutus; On the nature of gods; On divination; On duties*. University of Chicago Press.

Driessens, O. (2014). Theorizing celebrity studies: thickenings of media cultures and the role of (working) memory. *Communications*, 39(2), 109–127.

Du Bois, W.E.B. (1903). *The souls of black folk*. A.C. McLurg & Co.

Franck, G. (2019). The economy of attention. *Journal of Sociology*, 55(1), 8–19.

Gabler, N. (2000). *Life the movie: how entertainment conquered reality*. Vintage.

Gamson, J. (1994). *Claims to fame*. University of California Press.

Gamson, J. (2001). The assembly line of greatness: celebrity in twentieth century America. In: Harrington, C. and Bielby, D. (eds) *Popular culture: production and consumption* (pp. 259–282). Blackwell.

George, C. (2016). From bounce to mainstream: hip hop representations of post-Katrina New Orleans in music, film and television. *European Journal of American Culture*, 35(1), 17–32.

Gomez, M.G. and Astor, M. (2023). Who's running for president in 2024? *New York Times*, 29 August.

King, B. (2010). Stardom, celebrity and the money form. *The Velvet Light Trap*, 65, Spring, 7–19.

Lilti, A. (2017). *The invention of celebrity*. Polity.

Lofton, K. (2021). Oppugnancy in the New World: Charles Long considers KanyeWest. *American Religion*, 2(2), 87–102.

Lowenthal, L. (1989). *Critical theory and the Frankfurt theorists: lectures, correspondence, conversations*. Transaction.

Marcus, S. (2019). *The drama of celebrity*. Princeton University Press.

Marshall, P.D. (2016). *The celebrity persona pandemic*. University of Minnesota Press.

Marshall, P.D., Moore, C. and Barbour, K. (2015). Persona as method: exploring celebrity and the public self through persona studies. *Celebrity Studies*, 6(3), 288–305.

Marwick, A, and boyd, d. (2011). To see and be seen: celebrity practice on Twitter. *Convergence*, 17(2), 129–158.
Monk-Payton, B. (2023). The art of notoriety in Kanye West's persona. *Persona Studies*, 9(3), 21–37.
Pope, L. (2020). *Rap and politics*. Palgrave Macmillan.
Postman, N. (1987). *Amusing ourselves to death*. Methuen.
Richardson, C. (2011). 'Can't tell me nothing': symbolic violence, education and Kanye West. *Popular Music and Society*, 34(1), 97–112.
Rojek, C. (2011). *Pop music. Pop culture*. Polity.
Weber, M. (1978). *Economy and society*. 2 vols. University of California Press.
Wilson, B. (1975). *The noble savages*. University of California Press.

# THE CULT OF THE ENTREPRENEUR
## ELON MUSK

### WHAT IS THE CULT OF THE ENTREPRENEUR?

The cult of the entrepreneur signifies our idolatry of innovators, especially tech innovators. Our worship of the entrepreneur is underpinned by tech utopianism, society's faith in the capacity of technology to enhance and save humanity. Tech entrepreneurs are presented as disrupters, disrupting outdated industries and institutions. Enlightened technologists are purportedly driven by a higher purpose and humanitarian vision. They share faith that technology will lead to salvation and that startup culture is the best way to achieve this. Technological advancements and discoveries have made materials cheaper, mass production more efficient and accessible. The advances associated with inexpensive and lighter building materials have been undercut by expanding the scale and size of production (SMIL, 2019), yet we continue to evangelise technology for its philanthropic effects, believing that entrepreneurship is the most effective way to accomplish progress. Moreover, while most technological advancements involve collaboration, uncredited contributions, parallel developments and a series of starts and failures (Marwick, 2013), the cult of the entrepreneur reveres the individual innovator and investor as the source of social change. The entrepreneur is depicted as a guru and a visionary to such an extent that when we think of some of the most prominent tech brands over the past century, an individual entrepreneur comes to mind. The brand Apple has become synonymous with Steve Jobs; Theranos with Elizabeth Holmes and Tesla with Elon Musk; despite the fact that several of these companies were co-founded or founded by other people. To invest in these companies was to invest in these entrepreneurs. People attributed the success of the product and the company to individual innovators and investors, enabling these entrepreneurs to cultivate a movement of devoted 'true believers' who evangelise their brands (Hoffer, 2002).

Elon Musk exemplifies the cult of the entrepreneur. The South African entrepreneur and tech mogul simultaneously manages multiple companies in the US. He is the founder, chairman, CEO (Chief Executive Officer) and CTO (Chief Technology Officer) of the spacecraft manufacturer, SpaceX; the CEO, product architect and former chairman of the electric car and renewable energy company, Tesla, Inc.; the founder of the infrastructure and tunnel construction service, The Boring Company; co-founder of the neurotechnology company that is developing implantable brain–computer interfaces, Neurolink and the artificial intelligence research company, OpenAI; president of the Musk Foundation; and the owner, chairman and CTO of X Corp., a tech company which Musk established in 2023 after acquiring Twitter in 2022 for $44 billion USD. In 2023, Musk also founded xAI, a startup company working in the area of artificial intelligence (AI). The scope and success of Musk's business ventures have helped him to accumulate vast wealth; according to Bloomberg Billionaires Index, Musk is currently the wealthiest person in the world, with an estimated net worth of $232 billion USD. Musk's association with these companies depicts him as a genius, possessing extraordinary insight and superior intelligence across a variety of complex, technological domains. Although the success of an entrepreneur is contingent on economic growth, most cloak their ambitions in idealistic language about philanthropy rather than wealth (Marwick, 2013). When asked about his advice to aspiring young entrepreneurs, Musk replied, 'Try to be useful. To do things that are useful to the world and your fellow human beings. It's very hard to be useful' (Musk in Fridman, 2021). Adhering to this benevolent image of the entrepreneur, Musk's technological pursuits are presented as a form of altruism driven by a variety of different needs in a context of existential risk. Tesla promotes itself as a 'clean energy' company driven by the *need* to transition the world to a sustainable energy economy; The Boring Company is driven by the *need* to solve the failures of urban planning and mobility in Los Angeles, and SpaceX presents its ambition to colonise Mars via the development of the Starship launch vehicle as driven by the *need* to become a multi-planetary species to ensure humanity's existence.

The mythology of the entrepreneur is a constitutive part of Musk's brand. Similar to Elizabeth Holmes, Musk dropped out of Stanford University. For Musk, failing to graduate from college was not seen as a sign of failure, but rather a sign of greatness. Reminiscent of other successful entrepreneurs like Steve Jobs, who dropped out of Reed College to create Apple, and Bill Gates who dropped out of Harvard to focus on Microsoft, Musk believed he could have a greater impact through creating technology rather than learning about it. Musk's decision to drop out of college to focus on entrepreneurial pursuits resulted in financial success with the founding and acquisition of Zip2 ($307 million USD) and PayPal ($1.5 billion USD). Many of Stanford's most successful alumni were drop outs, who went on to found successful tech companies prior to graduating, including Google, Facebook (now Meta), WhatsApp, Snapchat, Netflix, LinkedIn, Yahoo and Hewlett-Packard. Located in California, much of the benefit of the campus is the social capital it generates for students, including their exposure to startups and local venture capitalists. *New York Magazine* described Stanford as, 'less a college than a kind of incubator or accelerator — a four-year networking opportunity for the next Systrom, Spiegel, or Thiel' (Read, 2019). In the venture-backed startup scene of Silicon Valley, increasing the visibility and status of the entrepreneur is a way to attract investors. Ironically, despite the growing industry dedicated to teaching and promoting entrepreneurial skills (Marwick, 2013), the cult of the entrepreneur builds on a myth about the unique attributes and talents of entrepreneurs that are often considered innate rather than taught. As a 2008 feature on Elon Musk in *GQ Magazine* explained:

> Once in a while, this planet gives birth to a child with freakish talent – freakish not only because it is vast, but because it is ready upon arrival, with batteries included and no assembly required. One need only open the box and step back.
>
> (Corsello, 2008)

Entrepreneurs are presented as brash, audacious risk takers, who bravely disrupt the system. By questioning convention and refusing to take no for an answer, they are depicted as gifted visionaries, who can predict the future and bring it into being. Hence, despite the complex, societal problems Musk's companies seek to solve, the cult of the entrepreneur presents him as a prodigious genius, who alone can solve society's most pressing challenges through entrepreneurship. The personification of the entrepreneur as a prophet who can individually bring about technological advances is supported by claims that entrepreneurs are revolutionary, free thinkers, who 'cannot work for anyone else.' In addition to their superhuman intellect, exceptional creativity and technical mastery, entrepreneurs are believed to be tenacious, revealing unrelenting devotion to actualising their vision. The unwavering focus of the the entrepreneur is alluded to by stories of entrepreneurs like Steve Jobs and Elizabeth Holmes, both of whom wore the same attire each day—a black turtleneck—so they could avoid decision fatigue and conserve their attention for company decision making. When asked during an interview if he had any advice to aspiring entrepreneurs, Musk replied, 'Work like hell. You have to put in 80–100 hours every week,' 'don't sleep,' 'work twice as hard' as anyone else (Musk, 2013). Musk frequently alludes to his dogged work ethic, recounting to *Bloomberg* how he slept on the floor of Tesla's factory because he wanted to suffer more than any other employee when the company experienced production problems with its Model 3 electric vehicle (Randall et al., 2018). Other reports claimed that Musk kept 'a white caseless pillow' at the Tesla factory that he used while 'sleeping on the floor under his desk' (Higgins and Pulliam, 2018). Together, these references to Musk's tenacious work ethic and devotion to Tesla invoke the impression of a superhuman genius at the forefront of technical innovation and steadfast in his philanthropic pursuits.

This myth making of Elon Musk also justifies the high expectations he places on his employees, who are expected to be A players or what Musk describes as 'hard core.' According to Musk's biographer, Walter Isaacson (2023), Musk values attributes such as excellence, trustworthiness and drive. He expects his employees to believe that the company's mission, 'is more important than anything else' (Isaacson in Fridman, 2023). Workers are promoted for staying overtime and working past midnight or on the weekends, which is interpreted as a sign of dedication and rationalised through claims that they 'would rather be burned out than bored' (Isaacson in Fridman, 2023). Musk's shrewd business ethic justified him firing over 80 per cent of the workforce when he acquired Twitter, those who he perceived to be neither useful and nor loyal (D'Cruze, 2023). The cult-like leadership style of Elon Musk has a legacy that predates the South African entrepreneur. Steve Jobs also employed a highly demanding managerial style reminiscent of those used by religious cult leaders; the entrepreneur's departure and triumphant return as Apple's CEO on the eve of the company's rumoured demise elevating him as the company's savior, as Alan Deutschman notes in *The Second Coming of Steve Jobs* (2001). Similar to Musk, Jobs' success as an entrepreneur excuses his well-documented 'ballistic temper' and the 'tongue lashings' he directed at employees (Siltanen, 2011). Revealing the religious aspects of the cult of the entrepreneur, Belk and Tumbat (2006) found that devotees of the cult of Macintosh do not see the negative side of Steve Jobs and instead revel in his visionary leadership. Similar accounts have been made about the cult-like leadership style of the US entrepreneur Elizabeth Holmes, who kept Theranos employees isolated from each other, staff turnover high and instilled what was describe as 'a culture of fear' (Lancet, 2002).

## WHY DOES THE CULT OF THE ENTREPRENEUR EMERGE?

Silicon Valley has become synonymous with entrepreneurship as the geographical region in which many successful tech startups have been established since the twentieth century. The journalist Don Hoefler popularised the term in a column entitled 'Silicon Valley USA' that he published in *Electronic News* (EN), a weekly periodical that covered the electronics industry, including the computer chip industry in the San Francisco Bay Area, in 1971 (Hoefler, 1971). The rationale for the name were the technology companies, located in the valley south of San Francisco, which used silicon to manufacture their chips (Morris and Penido, 2016). The computer chip industry emerged in Silicon Valley in the mid-1950s with companies such as Shockley Semiconductor Labs, established in Mountain View in 1956, and Fairchild Semiconductor in Palo Alto in 1957 (Lécuyer and Brock, 2010). These companies initiated a cycle of engineers becoming founders, as exemplified by the founding of National Semiconductor (1959), General Micro-Electronics (1963) and Intel (1968) (Vox, 2023). Although the Valley's association with technology was evident in the early twentieth century, in the 1950s accessing financing and employees remained a challenge. There were no venture capital investors in the area (Rao and Scaruffi, 2013: 96). The military often acted as the main funder and customer of technology companies (Leslie, 1993; O'Mara, 2019: 14). Silicon Valley's entrepreneurial spirit was aided by its proximity to industry and universities, such as UC Berkeley and Stanford, which produced not only research, ideas and students who became entrepreneurs, but emphasised practical, applied knowledge (McLaughlin, 2020). The creation of Stanford Industrial Park (renamed Stanford Research Park in 1970) in 1951, as a joint initiative between Stanford University and the City of Palo Alto, established a reciprocal relationship between the university and companies. Professors were encouraged to take corporate roles and companies could enroll employees as students at Stanford (Vox, 2023). In the following decades, companies such as Fairchild and Intel (1968) experienced significant growth and economic success, followed in the 1970s and 1980s by tech companies such as Apple (1976), Oracle (1977), Adobe (1982), Sun Microsystems (1982) and NeXT (1985). As Hoefler (1971) wrote, 'The pace has been so frantic that even hardened veterans of the semiconductor wars find it hard to realise that the Bay Area story covers an era of only 15 years.' Today, Silicon Valley remains a hub of technological investment and innovation as the home of Apple, Alphabet/Google, Meta, Visa and Chevron.

The development of the tech industry in Silicon Valley was influenced by the US counterculture. In the 1960s and 1970s, many young American hippies endorsed anti-establishment philosophies, rejecting mainstream norms and values (Baker, 2022b). Hundreds of thousands of idealistic hippies went back to the land, living collectively on communes, seeking self-sufficiency, autonomy and shared consciousness by practising alternative ways of living (Daloz, 2016). Despite being anti-institutional, hippies were not anti-technology. These 'new communalists' were anti-government and centralised authority, using technology and entrepreneurship as a means of living independently from the state and corporate system (Turner, 2010).

Many pioneers of computing viewed the decentralisation of the internet as an alternative to government and corporate control (Marwick, 2013) with the counterculture encouraging an ethos of creativity, individualism and innovation (Turner, 2010). In the 1960s, Stewart Brand founded the *Whole Earth Catalog*: a compendium of tools, resources and information for people interested in technology and self-sufficiency. The *Whole Earth Catalogue* was a huge success, selling more than one million copies from 1968 to 1972. In Steve Jobs' 2005 commencement speech at Stanford University, the founder and entrepreneur behind Apple Inc., described the *Catalog* as the conceptual forerunner of the World Wide Web and 'one of the bibles of my generation' (Jobs, 2005).

> When I was young, there was an amazing publication called The Whole Earth Catalog, which was one of the bibles of my generation. It was created by a fellow named Stewart Brand not far from here in Menlo Park, and he brought it to life with his poetic touch. This was in the late 1960s, before personal computers and desktop publishing, so it was all made with typewriters, scissors and Polaroid cameras. It was sort of like Google in paperback form, 35 years before Google came along: It was idealistic, and overflowing with neat tools and great notions.
>
> (Jobs, 2005)

The former editor-in-chief at Whole Earth, Kevin Kelly (2022), credited Brand with inventing the blogosphere, 'long before there was such a thing as a blog.' 'No topic was too esoteric, no degree of enthusiasm too ardent, no amateur expertise too uncertified to included.' Brand also created the WELL (Whole Earth 'Lectronic Link), one of the earliest online communities that featured message-board-style discussions on a wide variety of topics. The ethos of non-hierarchical collaboration developed on the communes from the necessity of shared resources and communal living (Turner, 2010). This culture of co-operation and sharing contributed to open-source software and the decentralised nature of the early internet, with the WELL extending this sense of community beyond the geographical confines of the commune. Some counterculture participants ventured into entrepreneurial activities involving technology. This often took the form of small scale startups, hackers and personal computer hobbyist groups (Marwick, 2013), which built on this 'philosophy of sharing, openness, decentralisation, and getting your hands on machines at any cost – to improve the machines and to improve the world' (Levy, 1984).

The counterculture shaped the entrepreneurial culture of Silicon Valley. The cult of the entrepreneur refers mostly to the culture of tech entrepreneurialism in the US. As the journalist Tom Wolfe (1983) wrote in his account of Intel's co-founder Robert Noyce, 'If you wanted to talk about the creators of the future, well, here they were here, in the Silicon Valley!'

> It was the 1960s and people in the East were hearing a lot about California surfers, California bikers, hot rodders, car customisers, California hippies, and political protesters, and the picture they got was of young people in jeans and T-shirts who were casual, spontaneous, impulsive, emotional, sensual, undisciplined, and obnoxiously proud of it. So these semiconductor outfits in the Silicon Valley with their CEOs dressed like camp counselors struck them as the business versions of the same thing.

This countercultural ethos found expression in technology brands like Apple, which despite being a large corporation marketed itself through the anti-corporate, anti-establishment, rebellious spirit of the counterculture. Apple's countercultural influence manifest itself in the company's origin story, logo (a rainbow apple), founders and employees. While 'IBM employees were known for their white shirts, clean-cut grooming, and conservative suits, Apple employees were known for their jeans, t-shirts, sandals, and long hair' (Belk and Tumbat, 2006), resembling the aesthetic of the anti-establishment hippie aesthetic of the time. However, despite Silicon Valley's image as a refuge for free-loving, spontaneous hippies, as Wolfe (1983) reminds readers:

> They couldn't have been more wrong. The new breed of the Silicon Valley lived for work. They were disciplined to the point of back spasms. They worked long hours and kept working on weekends. They became absorbed in their companies the way men once had in the palmy days of the automobile industry.
>
> (Wolfe, 1983)

Wolfe's description of the culture of Silicon Valley is echoed by more contemporary ethnographic accounts of tech firms in the region. In *Work, Pray, Code* (2022), Carolyn Chen draws on interviews with hundreds of employees from Silicon Valley who 'are finding their souls at work' to demonstrate how work functions as a form of religion for tech companies in the twenty-first century. In addition to tech companies operating as a 'faith community' and providing employees with a sense of belonging, meaning, purpose and transcendence, Chen (2002) notes that 'tech companies increasingly work like cults,' converting employees into to true believers and demanding loyalty and control over them (Chen, 2022).

Silicon Valley's culture of bold, disruptive entrepreneurship is intertwined with the spirit of late capitalism. Apple sought to disrupt personal computing, Paypal sought to disrupt how you pay for things and Theranos sought to disrupt medical testing. The revolutionary potential of technology is predicated on a culture of risk taking, driven by speed and scale. Investors are attracted to size and efficiency, encouraging entrepreneurs to move quickly, and refuse to let any obstacle get in their way. This prevailing culture of entrepreneurship at Silicon Valley is encapsulated by the aphorisms 'fake it until you make it,' 'move fast, break things' and 'the ends justify the means,' which allude to the entrepreneurial tendency to exaggerate or lie to investors about products and their company's growth (Lancet, 2022). In an article for *Harvard Business Review* entitled 'Entrepreneurs and the Truth', the authors noted that 'Enthusiasm can lead to exaggeration, exaggeration to falsity, and falsity to fraud' (Jensen et al., 2021). As one commentator explained when reflecting on the US entrepreneur Elizabeth Holmes, who was convicted of defrauding investors and customers by marketing defunct blood tests, the business model of Theranos was indicative of Silicon Valley, it 'played into group think of the moment [that] if you raised enough money and moved fast enough, success would follow' (Macnamey in *ABC Audio*, 2022). Musk employs similar tactics to publicise his brands. He continuously makes false predictions about the capacities and release date of products (e.g. 'full self-driving' (FSD) cars, SolarCity) to inspire confidence and investment in his companies (often before the finished product is produced). Similar to other Silicon Valley entrepreneurs, such as

Steve Jobs, who understood that their personal image was part of their brand's identity and played an important role in their pitch to investors (O'Mara, 2019), Musk's public persona is a constitutive part of his corporate strategy designed to leverage capital to specific ventures in the venture-backed startup scene of Silicon Valley (Ferrari Braun, 2023).

## HOW IS THE CULT OF THE ENTREPRENEUR ESTABLISHED AND MAINTAINED?

Most entrepreneurs achieve a cult following through their affiliation with a cult brand. Cult brands are 'a special class a magnetic brands,' which 'command super-high customer loyalty and almost evangelical customers or followers who are devoted to them' (Ragas and Bueno, 2011). Since the 1980s, building cults or brand communities has been a popular marketing strategy (Koay and Hernández Eriksson, 2006). Cult brands reflect consumers' commitment to a brand (Acosta and Devasagayam, 2010) and cater to people's need for security and belonging (Constantin and Stoenescu, 2014: 124). In *The Cult of Macintosh* (2006), Belk and Tumbat employ the term 'brand cult' to capture the extreme devotion consumers have toward certain brands and to explore the cultic quasi-religious aspects of this consumption. Apple is the epitome of a cult brand (Ragas and Bueno, 2011). Part of Steve Jobs' success as an entrepreneur was helping to create 'the Cult of Macintosh' (Belk and Tumbat, 2006). In addition to drawing on creation and saviour myths to elevate himself as the leader of the cult brand (Deutschman, 2001), Jobs used advertising to promote the belief that Mac users are unique, special and distinct (Constantin and Stoenescu, 2014). Early advertisements for Apple declared, 'Apple computer, the epitome of the American Dream.' Between 1997 and 2002, Apple used the advertising slogan 'think different,' as part of a billboard campaign that featured black and white images of revolutionary people and events – Einstein, Thomas Edison, Gandhi, and a famous photo of flowers placed in gun barrels during the protest of the Vietnam War – accompanied by the words 'think different' and a rainbow Apple logo. In addition to aligning Apple with revolutionary thinkers, the campaign distinguished Apple from its rival, IBM, who used the slogan: 'Think IBM' (Siltanen, 2011).

The billboard campaign was followed by a television advertising campaign, which used a similar aesthetic featuring revolutionary figures. A voice over by Richard Dreyfus accompanied the commercial:

> To the crazy ones. Here's to the misfits. The rebels. The troublemakers. The people who see the world differently ... The people who are crazy enough to believe they can change the world are the ones who actually do.

Apple's commercials combined the counterculture's anti-establishment ethos with eastern spirituality and western consumerism, promising to change the world and bring power and knowledge to the people through their various products. Apple's corporate branding presents the company's mission as motivated by more than profit (Belk and Tumbat, 2006). Apple consumers similarly saw themselves as more than 'consumption communities' (Boorstin, 1973) and 'subcultures of consumption' (Schouten and McAlexander, 1995), Apple's 'Think Different' campaign presented followers as rebels, who by consuming Mac products were participating in a revolution. These loyal consumers became brand evangelists for Apple who tried to convince others of their beliefs (Ragas and Bueno, 2011); a deliberate marketing strategy by Apple to foster devotion among staff and consumers (Belk and Tumbat, 2006). 'When the "Think Different" campaign launched, Apple immediately improved its profits despite releasing no significant new products. Within 12 months, Apple's stock price tripled' (Siltanen, 2011). Part of what makes Apple a cult brand is the company's emphasis on innovation (Belk and Tumbat, 2006; Constantin and Stoenescu, 2014: 124). The unveiling of a new Apple product by the company's CEO assumes a religious-like quality. When Apple launches a new product, crowds of people frequently wait in line, some of whom camp overnight. The hordes of Mac consumers waiting to purchase a new product are not simply a sign of demand, they are part of Apple's marketing strategy to create hype and interest in new products, propelled by a deliberately short supply (Kahney and Pierini, 2019). The media is central to helping cult brands attract brand awareness, attention and hype. Similar to Steve Jobs, one of Elon Musk's primary roles is to achieve media coverage for Tesla and exposure for the brand. Tesla is unique in that the company historically has not paid for advertising. Alon Leibovich, co-founder and CEO of BrandTotal explained, 'The brand doesn't feel the need to spend on paid social media marketing when their organic reach is so strong' (Koetsier, 2019). Instead, the company has become intertwined with the personal brand of Elon Musk.

The modern culture of creative entrepreneurship in Silicon Valley uses personal branding to achieve visibility and self-promotion (Marwick, 2013). There is a whole genre of books and podcasts constructed around the art of entrepreneurship through personal branding. Books such as *12 Months to $1 Million: How to Pick a Winning Product, Build a Real Business, and Become a Seven-Figure Entrepreneur* (Moran, 2020), *Zero to One: Notes on Start Ups, or How to Build the Future* (Thiel, 2014) and *Crushing It!: How Great Entrepreneurs Build Their Business and Influence-and How You Can Too* (Vaynerchuk, 2018), provide readers with practical, tactical advice about how to become a successful entrepreneur. Many of these texts focus on personal branding, documenting how an entrepreneur can build and amplify their personal brand online. These authors were inspired by an article Tom Peters wrote in 1997 for *Fast Company* entitled, 'The Brand Called You,' which claimed that 'everyone has a chance to be a brand worthy of remark.' The author and entrepreneur Gary Vaynerchuk (2018) made bolder claims, declaring that 'Everyone – EVERYONE – needs to start thinking of themselves as a brand. It is no longer an option. It is a necessity.' Personal branding is a set of marketing strategies applied to the individual wherein the person becomes the product (Baker and Rojek, 2020). Similar to a commercial brand, the 'self is viewed as a commodity to be sold to others' with the internet and social media making self-promotion possible at scale (Marwick, 2013: 166). Musk's celebrity image as a visionary genius – reinforced through feature articles in the media, cameos in films and television programmes like *Iron Man 2* (2010), *The Big Bang Theory* (2015), *Rick and Morty* (2019) and *Saturday Night Live* (2021) – provides new avenues for corporate advertising (Ferrari Braun, 2023). The internet has helped Elon Musk to amass a large cult-like following of fans who express intense devotion and admiration for him. Despite Musk's messianic status and the cult of fandom he has cultivated online, his followers resemble more of a brand community – 'a specialised, non-geographically bound community, based on a structured set of social relationships among admirers of a brand' (Muñiz and O'Guinn, 2001: 412) – than devotees in a traditional brick and mortar cult. The term follower is suggestive of cult-like thinking, and in today's digital environment many social media users are seeking to build an audience or online following.

Part of Musk's appeal is the microcelebrity status he has cultivated online. A microcelebrity is an individual who achieves fame online. The term was coined by Theresa Senft in her study of *Camgirls* (2008) to describe, 'a new style of online performance that involves people "amping up" their popularity over the Web using technologies like video, blogs and social networking sites' (Senft, 2008: 25). Microcelebrities cultivate a loyal following by appealing to niche communities and interests from tech startups (Marwick, 2013) to beauty and fashion (Duffy, 2016), health and wellness (Baker and Rojek, 2019, 2020) and politics (Marwick and Lewis, 2017). In addition to functioning as a noun to describe a category of people, the term microcelebrity operates as a descriptor of the self-presentation practices online users employ to achieve visibility and status online (Marwick, 2013). In *Lifestyle Gurus* (2020), we identified three self-presentation techniques microcelebrities use to establish trust and intimacy online. These include:

1 **Accessibility**: the impression of being ordinary and approachable.
2 **Authenticity**: the impression of being genuine and real.
3 **Autonomy**: the impression of being independent of corporate control and outside of the system.

Together, these self-presentation techniques convey the impression that microcelebrities are 'just like us' – aspirational, yet relatable in their apparent ordinariness. It demarcates them from traditional celebrities, many of whom are perceived as highly manufactured and remote in their skills, talents and achievements. The internet and social media also helps microcelebrities to establish trust and intimacy with their followers because it conveys them as equals who occupy the same online spaces, unmediated by agents, managers and editors – whether this autonomy is real or imagined.

Twitter has been central to Musk's microcelebrity status. In its early days, Twitter was perceived as a democratic medium (Turner, 2019: 143). Building on the utopian vision of the internet as democratic, participatory and egalitarian (boyd, 2014), Twitter's former CEO, Jack Dorsey, promoted the platform as a global public square: a space for 'hosting and serving conversations' (Dreyfuss, 2018), where individuals could express their opinions in public, build social networks and participate in the production of culture and knowledge. Views of this kind proposed that social media could revolutionise society and empower ordinary people by giving a voice to regular, oppressed and marginalised individuals. This techno utopianism was energised by a variety of social movements that took place from 2010 to 2012 – just four years after the platform was founded in 2006 – including the Arab Spring, the Occupy movement, the 2011 English Riots and Kony 2012 (Baker, 2014). A decade later Musk purchased Twitter, which he rebranded as X and promoted as the bastion of free speech. Although X has alienated many liberal users through its lack of content moderation and reinstatement of accounts previously suspended for promoting hate speech and harmful content (Kim, 2022; Lorenz, 2022), the platform continues to be central to Musk's cult-like following. Musk currently has over 160.2 million followers on X (formerly Twitter), making his one of the most influential accounts on the platform.

Twitter enables Musk to appear accessible to his audience. The low barriers to entry required to create a Twitter account permit Musk's followers – referred to as Muskites or Muskateers – to occupy the same online platform as Musk. Rather than relying on the mainstream media to consume interviews and sound bites about Musk's latest business ventures and technological innovations, Twitter made Musk accessible to his followers via frequent (often daily) tweets. Twitter expanded Musk's audience, but it also gave him *direct* access to his followers. Musk does not simply occupy the same symbolic space as his followers, he reads his replies and frequently responds to his followers and critics on Twitter. When Musk acquired Twitter, he created a series of Twitter polls to solicit his followers' advice on topics ranging from reinstating Trump's twitter account to creating an edit button and whether he should step down as Twitter's CEO. Musk has commented on everything from the war in Ukraine to treatments and measures to control

COVID-19. He has attracted attention by making a series of controversial tweets. In 2019, he tweeted 'Nuke Mars!' In 2020, he tweeted that 'The coronavirus pandemic is dumb' and in 2018 he referred to a British diver, who helped rescue a group of boys who were trapped in a cave in Thailand, as 'pedo guy.' In August 2018, Musk announced on Twitter that he intended to take Tesla private at $420 USD a share with 'funding secured.' His tweet resulted in the US Securities and Exchange Commission filing a lawsuit against the Tesla CEO for stating he had the funding for the buyout without providing specifics to support his claim. To settle the case, Musk stepped down as the chairman of Tesla and paid a $20 million USD fine. Musk is a polarising figure. While Musk's playful, irreverent tweets have landed him in controversy, the capacity for direct communication enhances the parasocial relationship Musk has formed with his followers.

Much of Musk's cult following is generated by his appearance of authenticity. Similar to the former US President Donald Trump, Musk's controversial tweets have helped him to build a cult following on Twitter. Like Trump, Musk does not consult a publicist to craft his tweets. He is impulsive and unfiltered, which fosters the impression of authenticity. Musk's followers relate to his unguarded, provocative and unpredictable demeanor. Musk's style of communication contributes to his impression as an uncensored tech maverick, who 'says it like it is.' Musk's impulsive communication style enables him to foster trust and intimacy with his followers because impulsivity is conflated with truth and juxtaposed with the calculated speech of political elites. Musk's provocative tweets are also a mode of 'attention hacking,' a tactic commonly used by far-right groups to increase the visibility of their ideas through the strategic use of social media, memes, and bots – as well as by targeting journalists, bloggers, and influencers to help spread content (Marwick and Lewis, 2017; see also Phillips, 2013; 2018). Each time Musk tweets a controversial opinion or meme, the mass media comments on the tweet, amplifying it online. In this regard, it is not just Musk's followers but also his critics that contribute to the media attention he receives. Twitter has enabled Musk to seed ideas that travel across the media ecosystem and give oxygen to his personal brand and companies. Musk continues to use the platform to make surprise announcements about new features and updates on his companies (sometimes in direct replies to users), which generates attention and creates interest in his brands.

Musk's use of Twitter has contributed to his appearance of being independent of the mainstream media and the political system. Social media enables microcelebrities to bypass the traditional gatekeepers of the mass media and entertainment industry (Baker and Rojek, 2020). In addition to making microcelebrities appear accessible to their followers, their microcelebrity status on social media fosters the impression of autonomy and independence of those who have traditionally controlled the narrative and the means of production. Musk's irreverent tweets are interpreted in this context as uncensored by the mainstream agenda. His impression as a truth teller who stands up to authority feeds into the early tech utopian promise of personal liberation through decentralisation (social media symbolically presented as a decentralised broadcast system, disrupting the highly consolidated media companies despite the centralised power structures of Big Tech). It is instrumental in his appearance as a trustworthy, credible alternative to institutional authority. Twitter has helped Musk to cultivate a loyal cult following of 'Musketeers' – mostly libertarian, white, male millennial fans who share his vision. In addition to their faith in Musk as a tech maverick and source of salvation, they look to Musk for wisdom on issues beyond technology, from solutions to the war in Ukraine to COVID-19 (Baker and Maddox, 2022). During the pandemic, Musk's criticism of mainstream politics has taken a more conspiratorial tone. His promotion of conspiracy theories involving Nancy Pelosi's husband and Dr Anthony Fauci, and his online trolling of competitors and critics, have helped him to appeal to a reactionary right-wing ecosystem.

## WHAT IS THE FUTURE OF THE CULT OF THE ENTREPRENEUR?

The cult of the entrepreneur aligns with core American values. Drawing on the meritocratic aspirations of the American Dream, the entrepreneur is presented as both self-made (Marwick, 2013) and an extraordinary genius. The myth of meritocracy is powerful because it assumes that anyone can come from anywhere and achieve success in Silicon Valley, if they are skilled and industrious

(Marwick, 2013). Conceiving of the tech scene as a meritocracy holds that those who succeed do so due to talent, creativity and character – elevating entrepreneurs above the masses as a unique, visionary class who deserve their success. The cult of Elon Musk draws on this mythology, aided and abetted by the media. Musk is presented as a 'genius' with 'freakish talent,' who is single-handedly responsible for progressive leaps in technology (Corsello, 2008). Just as Web 2.0 as a historical moment and an ongoing discourse combines technological progressivism – the view that technology always makes things better – and technological determinism – the notion that technology determines social effects (Marwick, 2013), the cult of the entrepreneur is driven by the view that entrepreneurial pursuits and startup culture is the most effective way to respond to social problems. Elon Musk's cult status similarly presents him as uniquely positioned to tackle the 'largest, most important, most difficult challenges of our time' (Corsello, 2008). Although the techno optimism of the late twentieth century has been undermined by a series of revelations and scandals involving Big Tech, much of the current conversation is about the apocalyptic potential of AI (Artificial Intelligence). Entrepreneurs such as Sam Altman and Elon Musk continue to capture the zeitgeist as superior individuals with the capacity to save or destroy humanity through AI.

The cult-like status of entrepreneurs raises important questions for cult brands. In their research on cult brands, Ragas and Bueno (2011) make a distinction between destructive and benign cults. They consider cult brands to fall into the latter category by fulfilling the 'emotional wants and needs of their followers in a positive way,' fostering a sense of community and 'personal freedom.' Cult brands are said to encourage non-conformity and rebellion against authority, 'demarcating the cult from the status quo' (Koay and Hernández Eriksson, 2006). This optimistic view of cult brands is complicated by the rise of microcelebrities on social media, who use personal branding strategies to spread misinformation, conspiracy theories and authoritarian extremism (see Baker, 2022a). Elon Musk's use of Twitter has increasingly fallen into this category. Similar to Donald Trump, Musk's Twitter feed is a combination of self-congratulatory posts, provocative memes and opinions, and right-wing talking points. Trump and Musk's impulsive, unhinged tweets are interpreted as signs of truth and authenticity that further enhance their microcelebrity, cult-like status. Both have repeatedly used Twitter to mock their critics, calling on their followers to amplify their derogatory messages. Although Musk's dedicated fan base does not tend to display the extreme characteristics of cults – isolation, manipulation and coercion – their online trolling is harmful and abusive. Despite social media's early association with democratic expression and participation, in these instances the medium has become what Fred Turner (2019) describes as 'an authoritarian's mouthpiece.' What remains to be seen is how AI will enable charismatic, personality centred modes of authoritarian entrepreneurship.

## REFERENCES

ABC Audio (2002). Crime and punishment. *The Dropout*. Available at: https://podcasts.apple.com/gb/podcast/crime-and-punishment/id1449500734?i=1000538306701

Acosta, P.M. and Devasagayam, R. (2010). Brand cult: extending the notion of brand communities. *Marketing Management Journal*, 20(1), 165–176.

Baker, S.A. (2014). *Social tragedy: the power of myth, ritual and emotion in the new media ecology*. Palgrave.

Baker, S.A. (2022a). Alt. health influencers: how wellness culture and web culture have been weaponised to promote conspiracy theories and far-right extremism during the COVID-19 pandemic. *European Journal of Cultural Studies*, 25(1), 3–24.

Baker, S.A. (2022b). *Wellness culture: how the wellness movement has been used to empower, profit and misinform*. Emerald Group.

Baker, S.A. and Maddox, A. (2022). From COVID-19 treatment to miracle cure: the role of influencers and public figures in amplifying the hydroxychloroquine and ivermectin conspiracy theories during the pandemic. *M/C Journal*, 25(1).

Baker, S.A. and Rojek, C. (2019). The Belle Gibson scandal: the rise of lifestyle gurus as micro-celebrities in low-trust societies. *Journal of Sociology*, 56(3), 388–404.

Baker, S.A. and Rojek, C. (2020). *Lifestyle gurus: constructing authority and influence online*. John Wiley & Sons.

Belk, R. and Tumbat, G. (2006). The cult of Macintosh. *Consumption Markets & Culture*, 8(3), 205–217.

Boorstin, D.J. (1973). *The Americans: the democratic experience*. Random House.

boyd, d. (2014) *It's complicated: the social lives of networked teens*. Yale University Press.

Chen, C. (2022). *Work pray code: when work becomes religion in Silicon Valley*. Princeton University Press.

Constantin, V.D.N. and Stoenescu, R.D.G. (2014). The impact of origin on creating a cult brand: the case of Apple. *SEA: Practical Application of Science*, 2(1).

Corsello, A. (2008). The believer. *GQ Magazine*, 31 December.

Daloz, K. (2016). *We are as gods: back to the land in the 1970s on the quest for a new America*. Public Affairs.

D'Cruze, D. (2023). Elon Musk confirms he has fired over 80% of Twitter employees so far. Available at: https://www.businesstoday.in/technology/news/story/elon-musk-confirms-he-has-fired-over-80-of-twitter-employees-so-far-377045-2023-04-12

Deutschman, A. (2001). *The second coming of Steve Jobs*. Currency.

Dreyfuss, E. (2018). Jack Dorsey has problems with Twitter, too. *Wired Magazine*. Available at: https://www.wired.com/story/wired25-jack-dorsey/

Duffy B.E. (2016). The romance of work: gender and aspirational labour in the digital culture industries. *International Journal of Cultural Studies*, 19(4), 441–457.

Ferrari Braun, A. (2023). The Elon Musk experience: celebrity management in financialised capitalism. *Celebrity Studies*, 14(4), 602–619. https://doi.org/10.1080/19392397.2022.2154685

Fridman, L. (2021). Elon Musk: SpaceX, Mars, Tesla Autopilot, self-driving, robotics, and AI. *Lex Fridman Podcast #252*. Available at: https://www.youtube.com/watch?v=DxREm3s1scA

Fridman, L. (2023). Walter Isaacson: Elon Musk, Steve Jobs, Einstein, Da Vinci & Ben Franklin. *Lex Fridman Podcast #395*. Available at: https://www.youtube.com/watch?v=aGOV5R7M1Js

Higgins, T. and Pulliam, S. (2018). Elon Musk races to exit Tesla's 'production hell.' *The Wall Street Journal*, 27 June. Available at: https://www.wsj.com/articles/elon-musk-races-to-exit-teslas-production-hell-1530149814?mod=searchresults&page=1&pos=4

Hoefler, D. (1971). Silicon Valley U.S.A. *Electronic News*, January.

Hoffer, E. (2002). *The true believer: thoughts on the nature of mass movements*. Perennial Classics.

Isaacson, W. (2023). *Elon Musk*. Simon & Schuster.

Jensen, K., Byers, T., Dunham, L. and Fjeld, J. (2021). Entrepreneurs and the truth. *Harvard Business Review*. Available at: https://hbr.org/2021/07/entrepreneurs-and-the-truth

Jobs, S. (2005). Stanford University commencement speech, 12 June. https://news.stanford.edu/2005/06/12/youve-got-find-love-jobs-says/

Kahney, L. and Pierini, D. (2019). *The cult of Mac*. No Starch Press.

Kelly, K. (2022). The Whole Earth Blogalog. Available at: https://kk.org/ct2/the-whole-earth-blogalog/

Kim, J. (2022). Elon Musk reinstates suspended journalists on Twitter after backlash. National Public Radio. Available at: https://www.npr.org/2022/12/17/1143796992/twitter-lifts-suspensions-on-several-journalists-amid-rift-between-the-site-and-

Koay, L. and Hernández Eriksson, I. (2006). A pragmatic approach to sustaining cult brand–case of Apple. Master's thesis, Department of International Marketing, MIMA International Marketing, Malardalen International Master Academy.

Koetsier, J. (2019). Tesla spends zero on ads: here's where BMW, Toyota, Ford, and Porsche spend digital ad dollars. *Forbes*, 6 May.

Lancet (2022). Theranos and the scientific community: at the bleeding edge. *Lancet*, 399(10321), 211.

Lécuyer, C. and Brock, D. (2010). *Makers of the microchip: a documentary history of Fairchild Semiconductor*. MIT Press.

Leslie, S. (1993). How the west was won: the military and the making of Silicon Valley. In: W. Asprey (ed.), *Technological competitiveness: contemporary and historical perspectives on electrical, electronics, and computer industries* (75–89). Institute of Electrical and Electronics Engineers.

Levy, S. (1984). *Hackers: heroes of the computer revolution*. Anchor Press/Doubleday.

Lorenz, T. (2022). 'Opening the gates of hell': Musk says he will revive banned accounts. *Washington Post*. Available at: https://www.washingtonpost.com/technology/2022/11/24/twitter-musk-reverses-suspensions/

Marwick, A.E. (2013). *Status update: celebrity, publicity, and branding in the social media age*. Yale University Press.

Marwick, A.E. and Lewis, R. (2017). Media manipulation and disinformation online. *Data & Society*, 15 May.

McLaughlin, J. (2020). *The entrepreneurs of Silicon Valley*. Audio book. Audible.

Moran, R.D. (2020). *12 months to $1 million: how to pick a winning product, build a real business, and become a seven-figure entrepreneur*. BenBella Books.

Morris, R. and Penido, M. (2016). How did Silicon Valley become Silicon Valley? *Endeavour Insight*.

Musk, E. (2013). Elon Musk: Work twice as hard as others. Available at: https://www.youtube.com/watch?v=GtaxU6DZvLs

Muñiz Jr, A.M. and O'Guinn, T.C. (2001). Brand community. *Journal of Consumer Research*, 27(4), 412–432.

O'Mara, M. (2019). *The code: Silicon Valley and the remaking of America*. Penguin.

Phillips, W. (2013). The house that Fox built: anonymous, spectacle, and cycles of amplification. *Television & New Media*, 14(6), 494–509.

Phillips, W. (2018). *The oxygen of amplification*. Data & Society Research Institute.

Ragas, M.W. and Bueno, B.J. (2011). *The power of cult branding: how 9 magnetic brands turned customers into loyal followers (and yours can, too!)*. Currency.

Randall, T., Eidelson, J., Hull, D., and Lippert, J. (2018). Hell for Elon Musk is a midsize sedan. *Bloomberg*, 12 July.

Rao, A. and Scaruffi, P. (2013). *A history of Silicon Valley: the greatest creation of wealth in the history of the planet, 1900–2013*. Omniware group.

Read, M. (2019). How to major in unicorn: many of the freshmen now arriving in Palo Alto came to raise capital and drop out. A cynic's guide to killing it at Stanford. *New York Magazine*, 4 September.

Schouten, J.W. and McAlexander, J.H. (1995). Subcultures of consumption: an ethnography of the new bikers. *Journal of consumer research*, 22(1), 43–61.

Senft, T.M. (2008). *Camgirls: celebrity and community in the age of social networks*. Peter Lang.

Siltanen, R. (2011). The real story behind Apple's 'think different' campaign. *Forbes*, 14 December.

Smil, V. (2019). Bill Gates' guru: 'I'm not impressed with Silicon Valley'. 'I don't have a cell phone'. 'I never blog'. *New Perspectives Quarterly*, 36(4), 54–59.

Thiel, P. (2014). *Zero to one: notes on startups, or how to build the future*. Random House.

Turner, F. (2010). *From counterculture to cyberculture: Stewart Brand, the Whole Earth Network, and the rise of digital utopianism*. University of Chicago Press.

Turner, F. (2019). Trump on Twitter: how a medium designed for democracy became an authoritarian's mouthpiece. In *Antidemocracy in America: truth, power, and the republic at risk* (pp. 83–92). Columbia University Press.

Vaynerchuk, G. (2018). *Crushing it!: how great entrepreneurs build their business and influence – and how you can too*. Harper Business.

Vox (2023). *Why Silicon Valley is here*. Amir Shapiro/YouTube.

Wolfe, T. (1983). The tinkerings of Robert Noyce: how the sun rose on the Silicon Valley. *Esquire Magazine*, December, 346–374.

# SELF-HELP CULTS
## ANDREW TATE

### WHAT IS A SELF-HELP CULT?

Self-help gurus have existed for centuries. The genre is commonly attributed to Samuel Smiles (1812–1904), who wrote what is regarded as the first self-help book in English, *Self-help with Illustrations of Character and Conduct* (1859). The book provided practical advice about how to achieve social and economic success. For Smiles, the key to self-improvement was to develop character and self-reliance. In keeping with the times, Smiles stressed the importance of Victorian values, including hard work, ingenuity, perseverance and thrift, encouraging readers to pursue self-sufficiency; a nod to the spirit of individualism that permeated Europe during the 1800s and inspired the transcendentalist movement of the mid-nineteenth century.[1] Smiles' text was aimed at young working-class men. The Scottish author and government reformer became disillusioned with bureaucracies' capacity to enact social reform. He came to believe that progress would emanate from new attitudes rather than from new laws, which influenced the practical advice he bestowed to individual readers about how to achieve self-improvement and their duty to become a better person. Despite seeking to help working-class men in Scotland to improve their conditions, Smiles' writing has universal appeal and speaks to perennial desires to achieve success and improve one's conditions in life. His practical tips, interwoven with biographical stories of

DOI: 10.4324/9781003335115-7

success, inspired people to take control of their lives. Although the advice espoused by *Self-help* shares much in common with the practical wisdom traditions and conduct manuals of the past, its individualist ethos was part of the cultural zeitgeist (Baker, 2022b: 86–87). Inspired by Ralph Waldo Emerson and John Stuart Mill, Smiles was one of many writers extolling the virtues of self-reliance, with self-help viewed as the key to social mobility and social progress. *Self-help* was a global success, referred to as 'the bible of mid-Victorian liberalism.' However, it was in the US that the self-help industry formed and flourished.

The self-help industry is a global phenomenon that grew significantly in the US in the twentieth century. There were several notable periods of growth. The first was in the 1930s, influenced by several texts in the early twentieth century. Notable examples include Wallace D. Wattle's *The Science of Getting Rich* (1910), Dale Carnegie's *How to Win Friends and Influence People* (1936), Napoleon Hill's *Think and Grow Rich* (1937) and Norman Vincent Peale's *The Power of Positive Thinking* (1952). The second was in the 1980s with the growth of self-help for women. Self-help was particularly popular in the US because it built on the ideal of the American Dream – the idea that anyone could be successful with discipline, determination and effort. Self-help literature endorses both a meritocratic vision of success and an individualist approach to knowledge that resists institutional learning. The genre's emphasis on self-belief shared much in common with New Thought and Christian Science with their shared conviction about the power of the mind. New Thought was a quasi-religious movement that coalesced in the US in the 1800s. Premised on the idea of the law of attraction, whereby 'like attracts like,' it proposed that the energy you project into the world determines what you attract in all areas of life from health, to wealth and relationships. The law of attraction is a common theme in much modern self-help literature, from *A Course in Miracles* (1976) to the best-selling self-help book, *The Secret*. It has replaced the common sense view that we shape our reality with the harmful view that we create our own reality, consequently victimising those experiencing structural disadvantage and misfortune.

While it is unlikely that many of these self-help gurus intentionally sought to cultivate cultic dynamics, the ideas they espoused have contributed to the emergence of self-help cults. A cult, as we have discussed in previous chapters, is a group characterised by a certain kind of power structure and internal relations of power based on charismatic authority. As cult researcher Janja Lalich (2017), elucidates, 'a cult can be either a sharply bounded social group or a diffusely bounded social movement held together through a shared commitment to a charismatic leader. It upholds a transcendent ideology (often but not always religious in nature) and requires a high level of commitment from its members in words and deeds. Most importantly, it requires a personal transformation orchestrated by the cult.'[2] According to Lalich's (2004) theory of 'bounded choice,' four interlocking dimensions comprise the framework of a cult's social system and internal dynamics:

1 **Charismatic Authority**: the emotional bond between a leader and followers. The general purpose of charismatic authority is to provide leadership. The specific goal is for the leader to be accepted as the legitimate authority and for members to regard him or her as someone special to be revered.
2 **Transcendent Belief System**: the overarching ideology that binds adherents to the group and keeps them behaving according to the group's rules and norms. The goal is to provide a worldview that offers meaning and purpose through a moral imperative.
3 **Systems of Control**: the network of acknowledged – or visible – regulatory mechanisms (rules, regulations, procedures) that guide the operation of the group. The specific goal is to create a behavioural system and disciplinary code that results in obedience and compliance.
4 **Systems of Influence**: the network of interactions and social influence that resides in the group's social relations. The specific goal is to create institutionalised group norms and an established code of conduct by which members are expected to live.

The combination of these four dimensions results in a 'self-sealing system' that exacts a high degree of commitment from its core members (Lalich, 2004). A self-sealing system is one that is closed in on itself, allowing no consideration of disconfirming evidence or alternative points of view.[3] A self-help cult is a group that encompasses these dimensions under the promise of individual empowerment and self-actualisation. The pursuit of self-improvement is central to self-help, with self-help gurus instructing people on how to improve their health, wealth and relationships or contribute to a larger political cause.

## WHY DO SELF-HELP CULTS EMERGE?

Self-help cults have flourished in the West following the decline of organised religion. The counter culture of the 1960s brought with it both a rejection of traditional religious doctrine and an interest in Eastern spirituality. This turn was not marked by the absence of religious belief, but a cultural shift towards New Age spirituality marked by a 'spiritual but not religious' identity (Baker, 2022b). The New Age combined Eastern spirituality with Western psychology. Unlike the austere doctrines and social conformity associated with organised religion, it offered practitioners the capacity to cherry pick their beliefs and practices with varying levels of commitment, which complemented the counter cultural ethos of the time. The US counter culture saw the proliferation of Eastern spiritual practices in the West, from yoga to transcendental meditation (Ingram, 2020). While some travelled to India to find a guru, new immigration laws in the US encouraged an influx of Eastern gurus to California, where they set up yoga studios, cults and communes.

The self-help cults that flourish in contemporary secular societies share this impulse towards liberalism and individualism. Practitioners seeking practical advice about how to improve their lives commonly seek a guru as a source of salvation and to help them 'see the light.' In *Lifestyle Gurus* (Baker and Rojek, 2019), we argued that the turn to gurus for self-help advice in contemporary secular societies is symptomatic of two conditions: (1) the decline of organised religion and the loosening of tradition, which has led to a state of 'ontological insecurity' (Giddens, 1991) wherein people seek guidance about how to live their lives, and (2) low trust society – not the absence of trust but rather growing distrust of institutional experts and elites; both of which result in people seeking alternative guru figures for wisdom and advice. The proliferation of gurus in the late twentieth century necessitates certain political conditions, such as liberalism and feminism, which permit people the freedom and choice to navigate their own lives. Self-help cults have also flourished in response to technological developments, including the invention of smartphones, the accessibility of mobile broadband and the shift from broadcast media (newspapers, television, radio) to social media, which has lowered the barriers to entry for content creators, enabling them to position themselves as self-proclaimed gurus and life coaches (Baker and Rojek, 2019). In addition to elevating certain individuals as self-help gurus, these new media technologies have intensified the cultic dynamics between these thought leaders and their followers and given rise to what can be termed self-help cults, as will be discussed in more detail below.

Self-help cults directed at men and women respond to specific economic, political and cultural conditions. Most early self-help literature was written by men for a male audience, with self-improvement the prerogative of men. Self-help texts written for women were mostly focused on the domestic sphere (Baker and Rojek, 2019). Since the 1980s, there has been a rise in self-help literature by and for women (McGee, 2005), reflecting a series of broader cultural, economic and political developments that enabled women to seek individual empowerment. The women's movement and the mass entrance of women in the labour market in the 1970s and 1980s contributed to a new subgenre of self-help literature to accommodate the changing roles of women. These self-help texts promised women they could have it all, as exemplified by Helen Gurley Brown's best-seller, *Having It All* (1982). The metaphor of life as a game featured prominently in self-help literature at the time (McGee, 2005). Books of this kind were premised on the idea that women could and should win at the game of life. But, as McGee (2005) notes, these texts were reactionary, proposing a vision of the ideal life modelled on traditional masculine 'versions of an isolated individual pursuing insular self-interest in the ostensible free-market of opportunities' (McGee, 2005: 83). The self was not pitched against the other, but oneself – encouraging women to be their 'best self,' as popularised by the self-help guru Oprah Winfrey. Self-help gurus proliferated in the late twentieth century with television and talk shows providing new avenues to broadcast practical tips about how to improve one's life. In the mid-1990s Oprah rebranded *The Oprah Winfrey Show* to help individuals achieve their own inner revolution under the mantra 'Change-Your-Life Television.' Similar to the New Age gurus that came before her, Oprah offered viewers an eclectic mix of self-help psychology, spirituality and consumption, under the premise of female empowerment.

The feminist movement led to a reactionary turn in male self-help, commonly referred to as the manosphere. The manosphere is a collection of blogs, forums, websites and online communities dedicated to men's issues. It is defined not by a single ideology, but brings together a variety of groups (including Men's Rights Activists, Men Going Their Own Way, pick-up artists and 'involuntary celibates' (incels)), which overlap on issues such as anti-feminism. These anti-feminists are critical of female empowerment and blame feminism for victimising men. They promote sexist beliefs, portraying women as inferior to men. The alpha male is revered as the natural state of man and the ideal embodiment of virile masculinity. Women, conversely, are depicted as submissive, emotional and weak, and subsequently relegated to the domestic sphere. Proponents often invoke the metaphor of the 'red pill' to describe waking up to this 'reality' about the essence of men and women. The manosphere has given rise to a series of self-help gurus focused on men's mental health, men's rights activism, and pick-up techniques. Many gurus have grown cult followings by speaking to feelings of male disenfranchisement, rejection and economic failure. Online influencers, such as Andrew Tate, are presented as an antidote to the rise of feminism in the twenty-first century, emerging as virile heroes at a time when aspirational masculine role models are obscured in the public domain.

Andrew Tate is a British-American social media influencer. He is a former world champion kickboxer who achieved notoriety in 2016 when he was eliminated from the UK reality television show, *Big Brother*, after a video surfaced of him appearing to beat a woman with a belt during a sexual encounter. Following the media scandal, both Tate and the woman featured in the video claimed that the act was consensual. In the years that followed, Tate featured in a series of provocative images and videos on social media. In addition to flaunting his wealth online – posting images of his luxury car collection, and travelling on yachts and in private jets – and sharing images of himself surrounded by bikini-clad women, Tate has regularly made brash misogynous and sexist statements, claiming that 'I see myself as superior to women,' 'I don't see women as capable,'[4] and 'Women … You get married to BELONG to and DEDICATE yourself to your man.' Tate has faced allegations of physical and sexual abuse from several women. In December 2022, he was arrested in Romania as part of an investigation into rape, human trafficking and forming an organised crime group to sexually exploit women.[5] In June 2023, Romania's Organised Crime Unit formally charged Tate with rape, human trafficking and forming an organised crime group. Tate has denied all charges against him and has subsequently been released from prison and house arrest while he awaits trial. Despite acknowledging during an interview that 'I am absolutely and utterly sexist,'[6] Tate maintains that many of his former statements have been taken out of context and were made in jest, and that he simply embodies traditional masculine values. Tate instructs his followers about how to achieve masculine excellence. However, unlike the practical wisdom traditions of the past, his advice is tailored to contemporary concerns, wherein 'the sexual marketplace has become globalised' and men must compete with men across the world for resources in the game of life.

## HOW ARE SELF-HELP CULTS ESTABLISHED AND MAINTAINED?

In the pre-digital age, many self-help cults began as self-improvement courses marketed as helping people to achieve self-actualisation and reach their full potential. Unsurprisingly, self-help cults of this kind flourished during the 1960s and 1970s across the US, taking advantage of the human potential movement and the counter cultural ethos of the time. Some of these cults were overtly religious and led by Eastern gurus who migrated to the US following new immigration laws in the mid-twentieth century. Others were more covert in their recruitment strategies, using personal growth and self-development courses as a front to recruit members into their cults by promising self-improvement and self-transformation. Today, self-help cults are thriving. They use professional associations, campus organisations, self-improvement seminars, leadership programmes and the internet as their main recruiting ground (Lalich, 2004). Cults of this kind generally fall under the rubric of self-help by promising to improve people's life across three domains: health, wealth and relationships (Baker and Rojek, 2019). Others recruit followers seeking to contribute to a larger political mission (Hassan, 2020; Stein, 2021). Many self-help cults initially take the form of Large Group Awareness Trainings (LGAT), offering personal development in a collective setting. These events lend themselves to cultic manipulation through physical co-presence, shared vulnerability and the charismatic authority of, and devotion to, the leader. The hierarchical structure of cults means that many members are recruited with a lack of informed consent (Hassan, 2021). By falsely presenting themselves to new recruits as self-improvement modules, cults like Scientology or NXIVM conceal themselves under the guise of self-help until members advance to higher levels, by which stage they are typically committed and coerced into upholding the cause. When self-help cults originate in a collective setting, they produce heightened collective emotions – what the French sociologist Emile Durkheim (1912) termed 'collective effervescence' – that are projected onto the guru. This ritualised behaviour, the corroborated physical and verbal sounds and gestures, and group emotions that follow, elevate the guru as a sacred object set apart from the profane – commonly exemplified by LGATs such as those offered by NXIVM and Tony Robbins. Self-help programmes provide an opportunistic gateway to cults because many use similar techniques to increase self-awareness and bring about self-transformation. High-arousal techniques, such as chanting, long meditation sessions, public confessions, loud or reverberating music, hypnosis and drug use, serve to shut down critical thinking (Lalich, 2017) and make recruits more susceptible to the leader's suggestions. In addition to elevating the status of the cult leader, these techniques lead people to believe they possess unique insight or awakening attributed to the leaders of the programmes.

Historically, cults have strategically targeted people experiencing situational vulnerability – the death of a loved one, divorce, job loss, moving to college and other periods of upheaval, change and uncertainty (Hassan, 2021). The popularity of the self-help genre in the western world provides self-help cults with a wider demographic to recruit from than do traditional religious cults. Self-help cults speak to perennial concerns such as how to achieve optimal health, fulfilling relationships and financial success. Those recruited via ostensibly innocuous self-help courses are often required to devote their time, money and energy more fully as they climb the hierarchy of the cult. Self-help cults commonly use coercion and intimidation tactics to discourage members from leaving the group. For example, Scientology and NXIVM, both of which initially present themselves in the guise of self-help, attempt to delegitimise ex-members and critics, whom they label 'suppressors.' It is this level of coercion that distinguishes a self-help cult from a group defined by a shared purpose.

The recruitment, conversion and coercion practices of traditional self-help cults differ from their online counterparts. The ubiquity of the internet and digital devices has lowered the barriers to entry for those looking to achieve guru status and a cult following in the twenty-first century (Baker and Rojek, 2019). Online cults are also free from the overheads required to establish and maintain a traditional brick-and-mortar cult. This has resulted in a proliferation of self-appointed cult leaders masquerading as influencers, entrepreneurs and gurus offering self-improvement products and services online. Cultic indoctrination has changed as a consequence of the internet. Classic modes of material control (behavioural, financial, relational forms of coercion) common in traditional brick-and-mortar cults are more difficult to achieve online. It is more challenging to control people's time, force them to work for free or separate them from their friends and family as is customary with traditional cults. In order to attract people's resources (time, energy, wealth), online cults must attract and maintain attention. We live in an attention economy, and the currency of the most successful contemporary self-help cults in the digital age is attention.

Similar to many self-help cults that proliferate online, Andrew Tate's currency is attention. Tate demonstrates skill at attracting and monetising attention. His controversial social media posts have garnered millions of views, going viral on social media and leading him to become the most googled man in August 2022, with more Google searches than those for England's late Queen, Donald Trump or Kim Kardashian combined (O'Leary, 2023). Provocative and polarising content is an essential component of how Tate achieves audience engagement and fame online. Many of Tate's social media posts are designed to stoke feminist outrage. In so doing, they appeal to disenfranchised men who feel as though liberals dominate the culture and that the system is unfairly rigged against them. Controversial posts are also a form of 'attention hacking,' a tactic commonly used by celebrities from Alex Jones to Donald Trump, and Gwyneth Paltrow's lifestyle brand, Goop (Baker and Rojek, 2019), as well as trolls and far-right groups, to increase the visibility of their ideas (Marwick and Lewis, 2017; Baker and Walsh, 2024). Journalists, politicians and influencers are strategically targeted by these groups to respond to their provocations, thereby shaping public discourse and inadvertently helping to spread racist, misogynist and hateful content online (Phillips, 2018). Tate, therefore, follows the standard playbook common to internet subcultures by taking advantage of the current media ecosystem to manipulate news frames, set agendas, and propagate ideas through algorithmic reinforcement (Phillips and Milner, 2021). When Tate's critics label him a misogynist and a danger to impressionable young men, the media attention and public scrutiny that follows only further elevates his fame online. Controversy also ensures that he remains relevant. We live in an attention economy and while many influencers are competing for our attention online, what makes Tate particularly successful in the context of self-help is the way he gains attention by making provocative comments then responds with generic self-help advice about how your thoughts shape your reality, how to shift your mindset and how to achieve physical health, which has broad public appeal yet would not be discovered amongst the noise online without his attention hacking tactics.

Much of Tate's fame centres on the self-help advice he offers to young men about how to achieve wealth creation and what he refers to as 'masculine excellence.' While his early content shared much in common with pick-up artists, since his release from prison his demeanour is ostensibly more measured. Tate preaches a stoic mindset. Resembling the Canadian psychologist Jordan Peterson, he speaks about the importance of discipline, duty and personal responsibility. He claims to be advocating for men's mental health – encouraging men to go to the gym, foster self-respect and stand up for themselves. However, unlike Peterson, much of Tate's appeal is his aspirational lifestyle. Similar to reality television stars and social media influencers such as the Kardashians, part of the mass attraction to Tate is that he portrays an aspirational lifestyle that many seek to emulate. He displays materialistic success and lives in a mansion with a fleet of rare, luxury cars, including his trademark Bugattis. Unlike many celebrities who have inherited their wealth, it is Tate's image as an entrepreneur and a self-made millionaire that is particularly attractive to his followers. Tate's origin story is central to his authority. Born in the US, Tate relocated to England aged 9 after his parents' divorce because this meant his mother would get more support from the state. Tate and his siblings grew up with their mother on a social housing estate in Luton, Bedfordshire. He explains,

> I was raised on welfare in Marsh Farm, which is the worst area of the worst town, Luton, with the highest crime rate. I went to a school with a four per cent pass rate, a single mother household effectively. Started with absolutely nothing, became a kickboxing world champion. So I started at the absolute lowest echelon of life and I would like to consider myself somewhere near the top now. I've been through absolutely every stage. So when I say to men you can become anything you want and my answer to you is masculine excellence, there is no other answer, I can't tell you how to rig the game … You have to get a better character to play this game of life.
>
> (Tate, in Carlson, 2023)

In an Instagram post shared by Tate's brother Tristan, he recalled being so poor that they would wait at KFC and salvage other people's leftover chicken to ensure they could consume enough protein. Tate's appearance as a self-made man is integral to his fame and following. Many of Tate's social media posts document his meritocratic journey as a self-made multi-millionaire. His capacity to overcome structural inequalities and achieve financial success is used to verify his principles and legitimise his brand: 'I come from absolutely nothing. I'm mixed race – my father was black and my mother is white. So, statistically, mixed race, single mother household, bad area. I ticked every box … to be a delinquent and I refused to be one.' The underlying message to his followers is that if he can rise above his humble origins to become a self-made multi-millionaire, they can too. It's all a matter of shifting your mindset.

Tate is unapologetic in his motivational advice, disparagingly referring to those lacking financial success as 'brokeys' and 'wageys.' Tate's origin story and visual displays of financial success online are used to justify his unapologetic tone. Resembling the impenitent approach of the US motivational coach and self-help guru Tony Robbins, Tate's recent twitter posts include statements such as, 'If you truly wanted money, you wouldn't be able to sleep until you fucking had it,' 'You're a loser because your mentality is loserish,' 'Depression is a choice. You CHOOSE.' Echoing Rhonda Byrne's best-selling book and film, *The Secret*, the self-help advice Tate espouses reminds his followers about the consequences of self-limiting beliefs and that their beliefs shape their reality. Much of this magical thinking has permeated self-help literature for decades. However, unlike the New Age text predicated on the law of attraction, Tate's message is more tangible because he has material evidence – the cars, the yachts, the watches and the women – that by changing your mindset, you can change your reality, and these displays of wealth are algorithmically fed to his followers on social media.

In addition to Tate's guru status, his business ventures have helped him to develop a cult following. Much of Tate's initial wealth was built from the webcam sex business, an industry he is now highly critical of and which he claims he hasn't been associated with for close to a decade. He offered a 'PHD program' – an acronym for Pimping Hoes Degree – featuring hours of video content instructing men about 'how to text women,' 'how your build your social media to pick up women,' 'how to test to see if a woman is high quality,' and 'how to get a woman in bed.' Much of this content was based on the emotional manipulation technique of negging (derived from the verb neg, meaning 'negative feedback'), where the manipulator seeks to undermine a woman's confidence and attempts to engender in them a need for the manipulator's approval, common in the pick-up scene (see Strauss, 2007; von Markovik, 2007). The programme is now defunct and has been replaced by other online educational programmes. One of Tate's major online revenue streams is derived from Hustler's University, an online educational and mentoring programme about wealth creation, rebranded as The Real World (TRW). TRW has the structure and dynamics of a cult. The self-help course promises young men the secrets of modern wealth creation and entrepreneurship for a monthly fee of $49.99.

Videos promoting Hustler's University with a voiceover repeat standard self-help memes, reminding viewers that 'everything is possible,' 'you too can live a #luxurylifestyle and #getrich by adopting a #millionairemindset.' In addition to providing the practical skills and knowledge needed to succeed in the real world (e.g. stock analysis, options plays, crypto analysis, e-commerce, copywriting, freelancing, artificial intelligence), members learn to cut, shred and repost content of Andrew Tate online.

Members of Tate's educational programmes are encouraged to recruit others to join via affiliate marketing links. Resembling a pyramid scheme, if someone signs up through their link, they receive a percentage of their subscription fee. The result is a single-level marketing scheme in which the profits are distributed between Tate and his affiliates. Legions of committed fans have set up accounts to promote Tate's content and link to his programmes. Tate claimed that his educational programmes recruit over 100,000 students a year, with reports suggesting that the Tate brothers accrue $5 million a month in subscriptions from their online educational platforms. In addition to accruing significant profits, Hustler's University and TRW have produced legions of loyal followers financially incentivised to actively promote Tate's brand and training courses online. They have made Tate go viral by consuming his content and reposting it via short video clips on social media, especially on YouTube and TikTok. This model is particularly powerful given that Tate was suspended from all of the major social media platforms (YouTube, TikTok, Twitter, Facebook and Instagram) until his Twitter account was reinstated when Elon Musk purchased the platform. Tate's followers disseminate his content online with savvy captions and hashtags, which make him impossible to moderate because it is his fans who are posting his content on his behalf (O'Leary, 2023).

Although the internet is central to how Andrew Tate recruits new members and maintains a loyal following, Tate's influence extends offline. Four years ago he created a secret society, The War Room (TWR), a fraternity modelled on brotherhood, virility and loyalty. Tate compares the private network to the Illuminati and the Freemasons, with TWR playing into male fantasies where members form a 'conglomerate of super heroes' – 'like the Avengers' – and Tate is presented as 'Batman.' Members include the Tate brothers and Iggy Semmelweis, a hypnotist who describes himself as 'the master of spells and shadows' and uses the power of persuasion (including NLP) in TWR (although it is not known how). New recruits are required to sign a non-disclosure agreement and pay $7979.00 USD to join the fraternity. TWR involves a series of Telegram channels on self-help topics (business, fitness, dating) and networking opportunities IRL (In Real Life). Those striving to reach the top tier of the cult must pay to attend additional courses and events priced at thousands of dollars each, and travel to Romania where they endure a series of tests designed to prove their worth; demonstrating that they 'deserve to be INSIDE.' This includes staged battles with professional fighters. Those who refuse to fight are publicly exposed to ritualised shaming. As a former kickboxing champion, Tate is positioned as an exemplar of masculine excellence to whom they ought to aspire. TWR is promoted as, 'a global network in which exemplars of individualism work to free the modern man from socially induced incarceration.' It draws on the vernacular of self-help, with Semmelweis maintaining that 'The War Room exists solely to give righteous and ambitious Men ALL the tools, contacts, opportunities required to become the BEST versions of themselves';[7] although a BBC documentary published after this chapter was drafted suggests that TWR is in fact a grooming cult whereby Tate's fame is being used to sell a method of abuse to men around the world at the expense of women (Tahsin and Shea, 2023). Tate offers his male followers a sense of meaning, purpose, identity and belonging in which he is elevated as an omnipotent messiah figure. His message to 'Get strong, work hard, get rich,' is appealing in a context in which rising inflation and the cost of living crisis has resulted in many working 9–5 jobs and unable to purchase a house or afford to raise children. However, Tate's emphasis on accountability and personal responsibility means that while he is referred to as 'Top G' and 'the commander,' he bears none of the responsibility if his followers are unable to accrue wealth and reach their potential. This is made evident in a disclaimer at the bottom of the site: 'Everything taught within The Real World is for education purposes only. It is up to each student to implement and do the work. The Real World team doesn't guarantee any profits or financial success.' Tate is not unique in this regard. Many self-help cults are legally protected by waivers.

Tate's promise of financial success is predicated on distrust of the system. Like many online gurus who have grown cult followings among alternative influence networks, Tate's anti-establishment stance is central to his populist appeal and fame online. Tate's criticism of the system occurs on two levels: (1) the systems that govern society are intentionally trying to enslave the public through conformity, deception and lies, and (2) these systems are trying to censor him for exposing the truth to his followers. Tate frequently invokes the sci-fi film *The Matrix*, to proclaim that we live in a false reality, where our minds are controlled and distracted to be used for 'the system.' He refers to himself as Morpheus, calling on his followers to resist the 'salve mind,' take the 'red pill,' wake up to the true reality of the world and escape the Matrix. When he was arrested in 2022, he claimed 'The Matrix has attacked me,' implying that he was the victim of a conspiracy because by refusing to comply he is dangerous to 'the Matrix.' This conspiratorial tone infuses much of his populist rhetoric about corrupt liberal elites controlling the global order. Invoking the persecuted hero narrative (see Baker, 2022a), Tate invokes opposition to an imaginary global system to strengthen group dynamics (Freud, 1921; Goffman, 1963). He presents himself as a rebel capable of 'helping men resist the slave programming' (Tate, in Carlson, 2023: 25:18), if they enrol in his programmes and adhere to the principles he espouses. Whereas the Matrix is designed to keep the masses poor and powerless, Tate presents his online educational programmes as an alternative source of secret knowledge about modern methods of wealth creation – 'They don't teach you how to make money at school because they don't want you to know' – which can liberate members from the elites who control the world and get rich at their expense. Unsurprisingly, these methods include alternative financial systems to fiat currency, such as Bitcoin and Blockchain.

Many join Tate's programmes because they fear financial insecurity, or being stuck in the Matrix. The irony is that it is Tate who is extracting and exploiting wealth from the public. The self-help cult of Andrew Tate is a hierarchical global network with Tate positioned as the self-proclaimed 'Top G' – an abbreviation for 'Top Gangster,' describing someone who is feared and respected by all. For Tate, the metaphor of life as a game extends to real life, where 'being a man is competitive' and life is a zero-sum game comprised of winners and losers: 'It's player versus player,' and according to Tate, 'You don't make money, you take money.' Much of the wealth Tate has reportedly acquired – numerous properties, jewellery, $400,000 in cryptocurrency and 15 rare luxury cars valued at more than £3 million – is derived from his affiliates. Characteristic of a cult, his online educational programmes involve coercion. Romanian prosecutors allege that the Tate brothers recruit, control and exploit women. In a statement, they have claimed that the Tate brothers recruited their alleged victims by misleading them with the 'loverboy method,' weaponising affection to lure victims into sex work.[8] Prosecutors allege controlling behaviour and heavy restrictions, including a ban on newly recruited women from 'leaving the house without permission, and needing to be accompanied by one of the Tates' trusted associates' (Williamson, 2023). This level of coercion extends to their online educational programmes. If a member decides to suspend or terminate their membership, they are ostracised from the social network and forbidden to return. They are relegated, as Tate explains, to 'jail' or 'the Matrix,' a type of purgatory where they are not only forbidden to access the secrets of modern wealth creation, but sent constant reminders of the financial 'wins' of other people enrolled in the programme. Even in TWR, Tate warns members, 'you can get kicked out at any moment without a refund.' It is also alleged that TWR encourages members to cut non-members from their life and that TWR leadership – referred to as 'generals' – strategically isolate women before luring them into sex work (Tahsin and Shea, 2023). Just as cults forbid disconfirming evidence or alternative points of view (Lalich, 2004), Tate uses his army of followers to silence his critics. Those who criticise Tate are challenged with a pro-Tate narrative by bots and followers who defend his brand. The self-help cult of Andrew Tate, thus, presents a timely example of a contemporary self-help cult, demonstrating how recruitment, conversion and coercion manifest online.

## WHAT IS THE FUTURE OF SELF-HELP CULTS?

Self-help is a billion-dollar industry. One would expect self-help cults to continue to flourish as technology affords online gurus new tools to reach audiences and offer practical advice about how to live. Guidance about how to improve one's health, wealth and relationships will undoubtedly change with advancements in culture and technology, but the uncertainties and longings the genre speaks to are likely to remain relevant. Modern self-help rebrands and repackages classical ideas in a way that is commensurate with contemporary epistemologies (e.g. an emphasis on scientific studies and concepts). The audience addressed alters based on who is perceived to have the capacity to reach their potential. The history of self-help is, thus, a history of social, economic and political change reflecting shifting notions about the self, agency and responsibility. Self-help has growing appeal in secular societies where the individual is seen as capable of self-mastery and lacks the moral compass of organised religion. Practitioners may identify as spiritual or religious, but these texts add little value in a world where individuals lack the agency and free will to improve their conditions.

Similar to Samuel Smiles and the self-help gurus who came before him, part of Andrew Tate's popular appeal is that he speaks about what it is to be a man in the twenty-first century. Beneath the veneer of machoism and the ostentatious displays of wealth, is a man speaking to a demographic facing change and uncertainty. Just as self-help texts written by women for women experienced a surge in growth in the 1980s as women experienced new rights and freedoms (McGee, 2005), questions around what it is to be a man are in a state of flux. Tate's message is appealing to men who feel disenfranchised in today's society. Harping back to the Golden Age of the post-war period when it was possible to live the American Dream with a house, car, wife and kids by following the rules of society, Tate provides a bleak vision of the average man's life trajectory today:

> I think that if you are a man, especially … and you decide to do exactly as you are told, you're going to end up depressed, in debt, working a job that you hate with a wife who doesn't respect you, with kids who don't listen to you, in a house you don't own, until she leaves you, and then you contemplate suicide a while and maybe you might find some purpose in the end, enough to survive and pay your taxes and then you are gone. I don't think a man who just follows the programming is going to find any happiness, but they don't care. Why would they? They don't have any concern with masculine happiness.
> 
> (Tate, in Carlson, 2023: 58:26–59:95)

By presenting men as victims of the Matrix, Tate provides an explanation for anxieties relating to financial insecurity, romantic rejection and low self-esteem. He also offers a solution. Tate is revered by his mostly young male followers as their mentor and saviour, explaining everything from how to find a quality partner, how to achieve physical and mental health and the secrets of modern wealth creation. Similar to the transcendent belief system comprising Lalich's (2004) theory of 'bounded choice,' Tate offers a total explanation of the past, present and future, including the 'path to salvation.' The solution is masculine excellence and the method for self-transformation involves adopting Tate's worldview, enrolling in his online programmes and proselytising his brand. In the current political landscape, characterised by distrust of social institutions, self-help – with its preference of self-discovery over official knowledge – is susceptible to populism and conspiratorial thinking. Just as the COVID-19 pandemic saw wellness culture become a gateway to conspiracism (Baker, 2022b), in the future we are likely to see a series of reactionary self-help gurus, using right-wing and populist talking points, to stoke pre-existing grievances, foster in-group dynamics and achieve a cult following.

## NOTES

1 The transcendentalist movement was a philosophical, religious and political movement led by the American philosopher and essayist Ralph Waldo Emerson. Together with other transcendentalists, including Henry David Thoreau, Emerson critiqued what he perceived to be uncritical social conformity, urging each person to find 'an original relation to the universe' (see Baker, 2022b).
2 https://ed.ted.com/lessons/why-do-people-join-cults-janja-lalich
3 https://psychwire.com/ask/topics/18yc6hv/ask-about-the-rise-of-selfhelp-cults
4 https://www.youtube.com/watch?v=2HzJvYkFNz0&t=2774s
5 https://www.bbc.co.uk/news/world-europe-65959097
6 https://www.youtube.com/watch?v=2HzJvYkFNz0&t=2774s
7 https://twitter.com/Iggy_Semmelweis/status/1647429274247499777
8 'My job was to meet a girl, go on a few dates, sleep with her, test if she's quality, get her to fall in love with me to where she'd do anything I say and then get her on webcam so we could become rich together,' he wrote on the page – which was subsequently taken down in February 2022.

## REFERENCES

Baker, S.A. (2022a). Alt. health influencers: how wellness culture and web culture have been weaponised to promote conspiracy theories and far-right extremism during the COVID-19 pandemic. *European Journal of Cultural Studies*, 25(1), 3–24.

Baker, S.A. (2022b). Wellness as a Gateway to Misinformation, Disinformation and Conspiracy. In *Wellness Culture: How the Wellness Movement has Been Used to Empower, Profit and Misinform* (pp. 115–151). Emerald Group Publishing Limited.

Baker, S.A. and Rojek, C. (2019). *Lifestyle gurus: constructing authority and influence online*. Polity.

Baker, S.A. and Walsh, M.J. (2024). 'Memes save lives': stigma and the production of anti-vaccination memes during the COVID-19 pandemic. *Social Media + Society*, 10(1).

Carlson, T. (2023). The Tucker Carlson interview has now moved to X due to Carlson's deal with the platform. *Andrew Tate X Tucker Carlson full interview*. Also Available at https://www.youtube.com/watch?v=84JXf5Sb0SY

Freud, S. (1921). *Group psychology and the analysis of the ego*. Read Books Ltd.

Giddens, A. (1991). *Modernity and self-identity: self and society in the late modern age*. Polity.

Goffman, E. (1963). *Stigma: notes on the management of spoiled identity*. Simon & Schuster.

Hassan, S.A. (2020). The BITE model of authoritarian control: undue influence, thought reform, brainwashing, mind control, trafficking and the law. Doctoral dissertation, Fielding Graduate University.

Hassan, S. (2021). Understanding cults: the basics. *Psychology Today*. Available at: https://www.psychologytoday.com/us/blog/freedom-mind/202106/understanding-cults-the-basics

Ingram, M. (2020). *Retreat: how the counterculture invented wellness*. Watkins Media.

Lalich, J. (2017). Why do people join cults? Ted Talks. Available at: https://www.youtube.com/watch?v=kB-dJaCXAxA

Lalich, J. (2004). *Bounded choice: true believers and charismatic cults*. University of California Press.

McGee, M. (2005). *Self-help, Inc.: makeover culture in American life*. Oxford University Press.

Marwick, A.E., & Lewis, R. (2017). *Media manipulation and disinformation online*. Data & Society Research Institute.

O'Leary, L. (2023). How Andrew Tate infected the internet. *Slate*, 19 July. Available at: https://slate.com/technology/2023/07/how-andrew-tate-went-viral.html

Phillips, W. (2018). The oxygen of amplification. *Data & Society*, 22, 1–128.

Phillips, W. and Milner, R.M. (2021). *You are here: a field guide for navigating polarized speech, conspiracy theories, and our polluted media landscape*. MIT Press.

Stein, A. (2021). *Terror, love and brainwashing: attachment in cults and totalitarian systems*. Routledge.

Strauss, N. (2007). *Rules of the game*. Canongate Books.

Tahsin, J. and Shea, M. (2023, 31 August). Andrew Tate: chats in 'war room' suggest dozens of women groomed. *BBC News*, 31 August. Available at: https://www.bbc.co.uk/news/world-europe-66604827

von Markovik, E. (2007). *The mystery method: how to get beautiful women into bed*. St. Martin's Press.

Williamson, L. (2023). Andrew Tate prosecution files reveal graphic claims of coercion ahead of trial. *BBC News*, 23 August. Available at: https://www.bbc.co.uk/news/world-europe-66581218

# THE CULT OF THE PUBLIC INTELLECTUAL
## JORDAN B. PETERSON

This chapter focuses on the cult of the public intellectual. It begins with a discussion of what makes a cult public intellectual, highlighting Susan Sontag as one of the defining twentieth-century examples of an intellectual who became a globally renowned cult intellectual. The next section discusses the fundamentally transformed twenty-first century context in which anyone aspiring to be a cult intellectual is required to function. For many reasons it is virtually impossible for anyone to attain this status. However, Jordan Peterson has done so and the rest of the chapter analyses his ascendance to formidable globally renowned cult public intellectual and how this cult status was attained, comprehended and sustained.

## WHAT IS THE CULT OF THE PUBLIC INTELLECTUAL?

There have always been powerful cults centred on the founding fathers of intellectual schools of thought such as Marx and Freud, who have been transformed into mythical figures with fanatically devoted followers (Stedman Jones, 2017; Crews, 2018). And there are also public intellectuals who Coser (1970) argues live for, rather than live off ideas; go beyond the immediate and the concrete to a more general realm of meaning and values; are concerned with core social values; grapple with pressing social issues; question prevailing truths and 'think otherwise'; exempt themselves from the ordinary requirements of everyday life; are at odds with their times; are able to convey their views effectively to a larger public; and need to engage in a 'play of the mind' for its own sake. For Alexander (2016: 343):

> intellectuals who enter public consciousness are powerful insofar as: (1) their ideas provide poetically potent scripts; (2) the scripts not only read well but have the potential to 'walk and talk,' thus contributing to the staging of social dramas; and (3) the enacted scripts so affect the meanings and motivations of audiences that social actors are motivated to participate in social movements and build new institutions. To the degree that these conditions are met, to that degree do intellectuals become dramatic personae in the deeply affecting performances their ideas have created. Their persons become iconic, condensed, simplified, and charismatic collective representations of the transformational models they themselves propose – contemporarily, in real time, or retrospectively, in memory.

No educational qualifications or expertise in a particular field are required to become a recognised intellectual of the public realm. They have, however, traditionally tended to come from the Left of the political spectrum (Nisbet, 2014; see also Said, 2002). When she died in 2004, Susan Sontag was mourned as:

> the intellectual plenipotentiary of American cultural life, militantly contemporary, insatiable in her appetite for culture and truly, madly, deeply conversant with every new development in fiction, philosophy, film and art. With the great turbines of her critical judgment turning, Sontag patrolled the latest edges of world culture.
> (Lacayo, 2005; see also Rollyson and Paddock, 2007)

The consensus was that Sontag was the only heavyweight American intellectual of the 1960s 'to survive in the mainstream, the only one to be read and argued about outside of academia' (Blue, 1983). And there was a strong sense that the death knell had rung for the cultural context that had created and sustained such an iconic intellectual persona (Jacobs and Townsley, 2011). Sontag developed a global cult following through writing thought-provoking books and articles; giving public lectures, taking controversial political stances, undertaking lecture tours; appearing on television and radio culture shows; becoming part of the university curriculum; receiving awards and by being talked and written about and photographed.

> She was for many a focal point – someone whom readers and commentators enjoyed revering, dismissing, complaining about, being exasperated, or infuriated, or amused, or electrified by – and she was a focusing consciousness; her stature as a writer and the value of her work have been, and no doubt will continue to be, debated, but what is beyond dispute is that she suggested, monitored, and even, to an extent, determined what was to be under discussion. She seemed to be at least twice as alive as most of us – to know everything, to do everything, to be inexhaustibly engaged. Her arresting appearance was familiar even to many non-readers from the photographs that recorded it over several decades and registered the glamour and magnetism – the sheer size – of her personality, and her celebrity was all the more potent and irreversible because the place she occupied was so far outside the usual radius of the spotlight. And also because it was a general combustion of her style, her brain, her concerns, and her looks – rather than any particular attribute or accomplishment – that gave off all that dazzle.
>
> (Eisenberg, 2008; see also Moser, 2020)

## WHY DOES THE CULT OF THE PUBLIC INTELLECTUAL EMERGE?

Post Sontag, aspirant public intellectuals were operating in a rewired digital public sphere defined by fame seeking, political paranoia, disinformation, conspiracy theorising, tribalistic identity politics and escalating culture wars. Lumby (1999: 37) noted that 'institutional boundaries which authorise and produce particular forms of knowledge' had been destabilised. This new generation included 'policy wonks', 'shock jock' journalists, 'change agents,' 'informers,' 'thought leaders,' 'rain-makers,' 'disruptors,' 'influencers,' 'thoughtifiers,' and 'motivators.' To transcend the noise, resonate and establish authoritative presence, an aspiring public intellectual had to be synchronised with the narcissistic performative logics of the social media ecosystem (Driessens, 2013; Keren and Hawkins, 2015) where, as Whiting and Williams (2013) note, people are browsing for a bewildering number of reasons: social interaction, information seeking, passing time, entertainment, relaxation, communicatory utility, convenience utility, expression of opinion, information sharing, and surveillance/knowledge about others. For Shea (2014), social media disseminates ideas to a broader range of people, but they

> also privilege some kinds of ideas over others, simplifying and flattening the world of ideas. They valorize in particular a quick-hit, name-branded, business-friendly kind of self-helpish insight – or they force truly important ideas into that kind of template. They favour the kind of idea that fits into our 'life hacking' culture: providing pointers or data that can be translated into improved productivity or happiness (often assumed to be the same). In subtler ways, this also affects the ideas that make their way to the public.

The podcasting revolution privileges the spoken word over the written word with discussions now occurring in a bewildering number of relatively unregulated echo chamber shows (Jacobs and Townsley, 2011). Nisbet (2014) notes how audiences increasingly expect a 'personal touch' to persuade them to engage with complex issues. Personality, appearance, voice, personal life, etc. were 'often (or expected to be) consistent with the subject matter they write [and talk] about, establishing with audiences their authenticity and/or a sense of commitment, demonstrating that they "walk the walk," "practice what they preach," or have acquired unique knowledge through exceptional experiences' (Nisbet, 2014: 811). Commodification, in the form of effective branding is also a critical part of the work, 'bound up with a dense web of promotion, selling, marketing, and financial transactions; endorser "blurbs" and social media endorsements, and the authoring of prefaces or reviews' (Nisbet, 2014: 812). In this social media ecosystem,

> the work of public intellectuals has the potential to 'catch on,' 'stick,' or 'go viral,' spreading by way of online spirals of attention driven by social media sharing and interpersonal

conversations. Articles are often pushed to prominence as the most popular, read, or emailed articles at the sites of the *New York Times* and the *Guardian* or magazines like *Rolling Stone*, which further expands their readership and reach. These articles are flagged, highlighted, contextualized, and spread by way of comments, Facebook 'like' buttons, and indicators of how often a story has been re-tweeted. Readership is further boosted through meta-commentary by bloggers and journalists at other news sites, and by advocacy groups who flood social media feeds with links and reactions .... these dynamics can transform the original analysis or perspective into a noteworthy political event.

(Nisbett, 2014: 812)

## HOW IS THE CULT OF THE PUBLIC INTELLECTUAL ESTABLISHED AND MAINTAINED?

Jordan Peterson was a relatively unknown psychology professor at the University of Toronto and a practising clinical psychologist. In his first book, the eccentric *Maps of Meaning: The Architecture of Belief* (Peterson, 1999), he examined myth and cultural patterns by combining Jungian psychology and neuroscience with anthropology, comparative religion and Biblical interpretation. Underpinning it all was an attempt to make psychological sense of belief systems and in particular the human capacity for evil, as demonstrated by the horrors of Nazi Germany, the USSR and Maoist China. This led Peterson to conclude that we need to oppose totalising ideological belief systems and ideologues. In this book Peterson explains how, in the context of the potential nuclear war, he had a complete crisis of faith, casting him into a personal hell with nightmares that brought him to near suicidal despair. Spiritual and intellectual salvation was achieved through managing to carve 'order' out of the 'chaos' of his life. Peterson became a media personality in 2004 with a TVOntario series based on his book and regular appearances as a commentator. It 'helped that he liked the camera and that the camera liked him back' (Doidge, 2018). He also expounded his views in two TEDx talks and in 2013, and understanding the promotional power of social media, started to upload his lectures onto YouTube. Peterson and colleagues also ran a website to deliver a 'writing therapy system' called 'The Self-Authoring Suite' to improve school performance and keep students from dropping out of school. It is also designed to improve people's physical and mental health.

Peterson's rapid ascent to 'dark web' intellectual stardom was set in motion in September 2016 when he waded into Canada's simmering culture wars. His 'Damascene Moment' was the realisation that proposed gender equity legislation would compel him to use gender neutral pronouns ('them' or 'they', 'ze' or 'zir') if requested to do so by transgender students or staff. In YouTube lectures and interviews he characterised the proposals, and the policies that would be used to enforce them, as the latest example of how:

- ideologically motivated legislation was being used to suppress the principles of free speech;
- truth and freedom were being bludgeoned by 'postmodern neo-Marxist' schemers who had taken control of universities and other cultural institutions.

Peterson warned that the legislation was paving the way for an even more Orwellian crackdown on free expression:

> There's only two alternatives to that. One is silent slavery with all the repression and resentment that that will generate, and the other is outright conflict. Free speech is not just another value. It's the foundation of Western civilization.
> (BBC, 4 November 2016)

Self-profiling as a proponent of unrestricted free expression, the radicalised professor adopted a martyr's position, declaring that he would be willing to be dismissed from his tenured university position and/or be imprisoned. He also warned

> that the continual careless pushing of people by left wing radicals is dangerously waking up the right wing. *So you can consider this a prophecy from me if you want.* Inside the collective is a beast

and the beast uses its fists. If you wake up the beast then violence emerges. I'm afraid that this continual pushing by radical left wingers is going to wake up the beast.

(CBC Radio, 30 September 2016)

A recorded confrontation in October 2016 between an excitable Peterson and transgender activists who were accusing him of provoking a 'hate storm' went viral. Peterson had 'hit a hornets' nest at the most propitious time' (Spears, 2017; see also Black, 2021). The resultant media frenzy transformed him into the most polarising figure in Canada. For his supporters, footage of the repeated attempts to shut him down at a 'Rally for Free Speech' provided 'irrefutable proof' that free expression was under siege from ideological fanatics. He was vilified by his detractors as 'a gateway drug to the sprawling red-pilled netherworld of men's-rights activism, scientific racism, and revanchist white ethnonationalism' (Yang, 2018). Peterson became involved in the case of Lindsay Shepherd, a graduate teacher at Wilfred Laurier University, Ontario, who was censored for playing a video clip of his views to her students. After Shepherd leaked her covertly recorded disciplinary meeting to the media, the university was forced to issue a public apology to her. Peterson then threatened to sue the university and two members of staff for defamation.

In lectures and videos, numerous news show appearances, pointed Q&A sessions and interviews and conversations Peterson hardened his profile as an energetic culture warrior. He excoriated his arch enemies, the 'postmodern neo-Marxists' schemers, who he claimed had infiltrated all aspects of cultural and political life and weaponised identity politics to create chaos (Cussen, 2022). Peterson was recycling 'forgotten' right-wing engagements in the culture wars that had marked the 1980s and 1990s (Hartman, 2019; Kimmel and Ferber, 2000). He called for the defunding of universities that did not publicly evidence their commitment to free speech and subsequently declared that he would create a data base of 'postmodern neo-Marxist' university courses, academics and disciplines that could be avoided by students.

Peterson's evangelising echoed across an 'intellectual dark web' (IDW) that consisted of 'a collection of iconoclastic thinkers, academic renegades and media personalities who are having a rolling conversation – on podcasts, YouTube and Twitter, and in sold-out auditoriums – that sound unlike anything else happening, at least publicly, in the culture right now' (Weiss, 2018; Hawley, 2018; Hamburger, 2018; Brooks, 2020). Followers wishing to actively support Peterson were given another outlet when from 2017 Peterson used the crowdfunding site Patreon to fund his activities in exchange for exclusive Q&A sessions, online tutorials and pep talks. At one point he was making $80,000 a month on Patreon.

> I shouldn't say this, but I'm going to, because it's just so goddamn funny I can't help but say it: I've figured out how to monetize social justice warriors .... If they let me speak, then I get to speak, and then I make more money on Patreon ... if they protest me, then that goes up on YouTube, and my Patreon account goes WAY up.
>
> (Beauchamp, 2018)

Google's dismissal of James Damore, one of its software engineers, in 2017 for challenging the company's stifling 'ideological echo chamber' and its gender and diversity policies, enabled Peterson to widen his attack, claiming that Silicon Valley was in thrall to political correctness.

By the time his self-help 'gospel,' *12 Rules for Life: An Antidote to Chaos* was published in 2018, Peterson was already a cult figure with an online congregation of an estimated 800,000 on Twitter and 1.4 million on YouTube (Beauchamp, 2018) who were promoting his salvation and damnation scenarios. The salvation scenario was that it was still possible to reassert: the redemptive power of the individual; the sanctity of truth; the right to freedom of expression and the West's intellectual and spiritual heritage. The damnation scenario was a nightmarish future resultant from incorrigible 'postmodern neo-Marxist' schemers successfully imposing their totalitarian agenda or provoking an extreme right wing backlash.

Peterson became a player in the lucrative market for self-help books. Unlike the others, his multi-million best-selling 'gospel' was made up of a hotchpot of personal anecdotes, practical advice, homilies, euphemisms, theological quotations, archetypal examples drawn from Jung, Nietzschean references, historical illustrations, psychotherapy and neuroscience. His 'gospel' reiterated his overarching thesis that the eternal struggle between the primal constituents of 'order' and 'chaos' and the mediating process of 'consciousness,' constitute 'the world of experience' (Peterson, 2018: 35). The good news is that 'chaos' can be managed through leading orderly, purposeful, lives, staying on the 'straight and narrow path' and heroically shouldering as much personal responsibility as possible. The bad news is that the alternative is damnation in 'the most barren, hopeless and malevolent subdivision of the underworld of chaos, where disappointed and resentful people forever dwell' (Peterson, 2018: 220). The 'gospel' also laid out fundamental truths:

- ancient archetypal myths;
- the transcendent truths of Judeo-Christian ethics;
- biologically determined sex differences;
- patriarchy;
- the traditional heteronormative family and its child rearing skills;
- the gendered division of labour;
- dominance hierarchies;
- free market enterprise.

The 12 self-help precepts were meant to be a general antidote to chaos whilst also being directed at a male audience, particularly young men. The damnation news, according to Peterson, was this was the group who was really 'suffering' and had their backs against the wall in contemporary society. They had to learn to survive the anguish of being part of competitive male hierarchies as well as coping with paranoid parenting and being under siege by an overarching feminist project intent on emasculating them:

> as privileged beneficiaries of the patriarchy, as possible adherents to rape culture, they're sexually suspect. Their ambitions make them plunderers of the planet. They're not welcome.
>
> (2018: 297)

White boys, Peterson claimed, had been further weakened by being labelled as irredeemable racists. The salvation news was that deliverance was at hand. A rugged individualist coaching regime would end the unwarranted suffering, enabling boys to transition to a self-confident, self-reliant version of manhood. He demanded that men should 'man up,' find their best selves and take the 'heroic' path: standing up straight, accepting personal responsibility; eschewing self-deception; ditching the culture of victimization and resentment; self-reliance, self-competence, self-discipline, telling the truth, challenging falsehoods, acting in good faith, taking risks, being heroic, developing a vision, avoiding loser friends, pushing back against enemies, and speak the truth. They were also advised to start with their own 'Being,' tidying up their rooms before attempting to re-order society or the planet. Men could find inspiration in the life of 'the victorious lobster, with its 350 million years of practical wisdom.' Peterson also included a warning for feminists: 'if you think tough men are dangerous, wait until you see what weak men are capable of' (2018: 332). Relentless guilt tripping was pushing men too far, increasing both antagonism between the sexes and the risks of a backlash.

The broader significance of Peterson's 'gospel' lay in the phenomenal global sales in more than 50 languages and the positive coverage that it generated (Bush, 2018). He had crossed over into mainstream public life where he was able to project an image as a dapper Canadian psychologist with a distinctive voice, theatrical flair and personal integrity who had provocative views on all the hot button issues (Beauchamp, 2018; MacDougald, 2018). Despite the vociferous efforts of his detractors to label Peterson either as a kook or an incendiary alt-right provocateur (Bowles, 2018; Lynskey, 2018; Mishra, 2018) he metastasised into a cultural phenomenon – scientist, clinician, edutainer, revivalist preacher, spiritual guide, philosopher, truth-telling seer – see sawing across numerous screens and platforms. He also, in his own distinctive way, met Coser (1970) and Alexander's (2016) definition of a public intellectual.

The mainstream media promoted Peterson's 'gospel,' running book reviews, interviews, profiles and op-eds that elevated his public profile. He was extolled as: 'the most influential public intellectual in the Western world right now' (*New York Times*, 2018); 'The first mega-intellectual celebrity of the social-media era' (*Harpers Review*); 'fast becoming the closest that academia has to a rock star' (*The Observer*); 'a prophet for our times' (*New Statesman*); 'Peterson is a new kind of public intellectual, using YouTube to spread ideas infinitely wider than predecessors such as Bertrand Russell or Isaiah Berlin' (Rajan, 2018); 'one of the most talked about, polarising intellectuals in the world' (*Sydney Morning Herald*); 'a kind of secular prophet' (*The Times*) 'an entirely new model of the public intellectual, halfway between Marcus Aurelius and Martha Stewart' (*Guardian*); 'the most significant conservative thinker to appear in the English-speaking world in a generation' (*Wall Street Journal*); 'the hottest intellectual in the Western world today' (*South China Morning Post*).

Peterson mania was amplified as a result of

- interviews with Cathy Newman on Channel 4 in January 2018, Bari Weiss at the Aspen Ideas Festival in June and Helen Lewis in GQ magazine later that year. The Newman interview went viral with more than 6 million views on YouTube within one month;
- the University of Cambridge revoking his planned visiting fellowship at the divinity faculty in April 2019. This was because the university had been notified of a photograph of Peterson posing with a supporter who was wearing an anti-Islamic t-shirt;
- Slavoj Žižek providing him with a novel platform in a 'Happiness: Capitalism vs Marxism' debate of the century' in April 2019;
- the launch of 'Thinkspot,' an 'anti-censorship … intellectual playground for censorship-free discourse';
- the release of the documentary 'Shut Him Down: The Rise of Jordan Peterson.'

The fact that Peterson's global book promotion events had attracted more than 250,000 people in 100 different cities was also posing the burning question: why was Peterson attracting such a large cult following? Amongst commentators, there was general agreement that his sold out events resembled salvationist gatherings with the congregation in awe to a preacher who brought the storm down (Lynsky, 2018). Peterson, the austere father figure, had found a remarkably receptive audience amongst jaded young men in particular who were craving direction in order to live meaningful and purposeful lives (Brooks, 2018; Burton, 2018; Law, 2018; Lewis, 2021; Lynskey, 2018; Roberts, 2018; Robinson, 2018; Yang, 2018). His talks were attracting desperate souls who nobody else cared about.

> They're hungry for a discussion for the relationship between responsibility and meaning. We haven't had that in our culture for 50 years. We've concentrated on rights and privileges, freedom and compulsive pleasure. Those are useful in their place but they're shallow and that's not good because if people are moored shallowly then their storms wreck them and storms come along. So I'm talking to people about how they can build a foundation beneath them that works and people need to know that.

From the outset Peterson established an extraordinary 'Dad-like' intimate, authentic familiarity with his ever expanding online congregation. It became closely intertwined with his life, privy to his personal journey to intellectual and spiritual transformation, his home life, his trials and tribulations, including grappling with bouts of depression and an auto-immune disorder, his personal faith, his histrionics, daffy clothing choices, his favourite books, his diet, the strains of celebritydom, his demonisation and absorbing the 'suffering' of the 'truly neglected.' Between motivational 'toughen up, weasels' pep talks, Peterson also assured his online congregation that the rules were for him as well as everyone else and that he continually fell short on sticking to them. Members also shared 'treasured moments' when they would see/hear him take their opinions into account, 'beasting' his arch enemies and when he was moved to tears in interviews and presentations. A remarkable interview in September 2019 saw a choked up Peterson seemingly on the edge of a breakdown as he reflected on stardom, becoming a hate figure and the relationship with his followers that was

> difficult to both understand and to tolerate because I've been opened up to the trouble that people have far in excess of what I've experienced as a clinical psychologist … To get a taste of the despair that can be ameliorated with not much more you know

than some words of encouragement, some statement that you as a human being are not intrinsically worthless and you have a spirit worth preserving and the things you do in your life correctly are important. People are literally dying for lack of that. I mean that honestly. I don't know how many people have told me these very hard things to hear. It's been hundreds of people … who have told me they are still alive because they watched my lectures or read my book.

To the consternation of his congregation and the joy of his opponents Peterson unexpectedly disappeared from public view in late 2019 (Beyerstein, 2020). It subsequently transpired that in this chaotic period of his life he had nearly died in hospital in Russia following dependency on anti-anxiety pills. From mid-2020 Peterson made a 'miraculous' re-appearance, assuring his online congregation that he had been saved. His plans for the future included a new video series on the Bible, joining the *Daily Wire* and publishing the next part of his gospel, *Beyond Order: 12 More Rules for Life*. Re-energised, he also resumed his cultural warrior work with invectives against 'toxic femininity,' transgender activists, Islam, 'Big Pharma,' the 'COVID scam' and the 'tyranny' of lockdowns, the Ukraine war, and promoting the views of climate crisis denialists. In August 2023 an Ontario court required him to complete a 'professionalism in public statements' coaching programme or risk losing his professional practice license from the Ontario College of Psychologists. This followed a series of complaints about 'degrading, demeaning' tweets Peterson had posted which were undermining public trust in the profession and raising questions about his ability to 'appropriately carry out his responsibilities as a registered psychologist.' He once more assumed the martyr's role, saying that the court ruling provided further proof that there was an establishment conspiracy to stop him from speaking the truth (Peterson, 2024).

## WHAT IS THE FUTURE OF THE CULT PUBLIC INTELLECTUAL?

Jordan B. Peterson is an intriguing case study of how social media has changed the way a cult leader's charisma and followership works in the twenty-first century 'public sphere.' The medium was the springboard for his extraordinary rise from acerbic academic to revered/reviled culture warrior to global cult intellectual guru. Since the mid-2000s the promotional and performative power of social media has been leveraged to maximum effect to fashion his combative 'truth-teller' counterpoint to 'postmodern neo-Marxist' schemers and their fellow travellers. Peterson was a YouTube pioneer who used the channel to comment on hotly contested social issues and spread his salvationist gospel far and wide in collaboration with IDW networks. Fully intermediatised, he cultivated charismatic relationships with his online congregation, a section of whom are willing to transform his books into best sellers and attend salvationist events. Peterson has many of the attributes of a classic cult leader. Messianic and charismatic, he has demonstrated the online and offline ability to cultivate, retain and grow a devoted congregation in the face of vitriolic opposition. The control he exercises over his congregation is achieved not through coercion but through the classic promise of spiritual enlightenment and empowerment. Peterson's bonds with his congregation and his cult leader credentials are also electrified by his unflinching willingness to pick fights with his 'arch-enemies.' Tireless promotion of his tough love 'gospel' turbo-charged Peterson's status to that of a globally resonating cult intellectual:

- critically appreciated by the mainstream media;
- cementing his status as a leading traditionalist;
- converting a wider constituency of mainline conservatives and libertarians who were seeking an intellectual figurehead with mass appeal;
- triggering the curiosity of a variety of religious commentators;
- amplifying his standing with his own congregation;
- and ratcheting up the 'WTF' fury of his 'arch enemies.'

However, in line with his *24 Rules*, Peterson has always been willing to play 'a more difficult game' of self-transformation. The next stage of his heroic journey is metamorphosing into a visionary leader not just of the IDW and his congregation but of an international cultural conservative movement. In January 2023 he announced that he was part of a group that had established 'The Alliance for Responsible Citizenship' (the ARC) as an antidote to the 'Great Reset' proposed by the World Economic Forum (WEF). ARC is a neo-conservative call to action with its vision of 'offering hope in the age of the permacrisis.'

In evangelical talks, interviews and articles to publicise the first ARC conference in late 2023, Peterson laid out his salvation and damnation scenarios. The salvation scenario is that humanity is blessed to live in a relatively peaceful age of 'expanding abundance' and unlimited opportunity. The damnation scenario is that Western societies are engulfed by 'existential chaos.' He continues to insist that 'postmodern neo-Marxism' is undermining faith in the Western values and traditions and institutional arrangements necessary to unite and guide. Equally significantly, according to Peterson, eco-fanatics, such as the WEF, are scaring people into acquiescing to both their humanity-threatening climate change agenda and the introduction of new forms of 'global-corporate-fascist-government-media' control. He is now firmly aligned with horse shoe conspiracy theorists who are obsessed with revealing the sinister goals of the 'globalists' who are championing the 'Great Reset.' However, in his most ambitious play to date, he is attempting to galvanise a broad church of people of 'good will and good sense' who will sign up to his on-going messianic mission to tilt the world 'towards heaven and away from hell.' In so doing he is also developing the template of how to become a global cult intellectual leader in the digital 'public sphere.'

## REFERENCES

Alexander, J. (2016). Dramatic intellectuals. *International Journal of Political Cultural Sociology*, 29, 341–358.

Atlas. J. (1985). The changing world of New York intellectuals. *New York Times*, 25 August.

Baggini, J. (2018). 12 rules for life by Jordan Peterson. *Financial Times*, 17 January.

Basaure, M., Joignant, A. and Théodore, R. (2023). Public intellectuals in digital and global times: the case of Project Syndicate. *International Journal of Politics, Culture and Society*, 36, 139–161.

Beauchamp, Z. (2018). The obscure Canadian psychologist turned right wing celebrity, explained. *Vox*, 21 May.

Beyerstein, L. (2020). What happened to Jordan Peterson? *Critical Mass*, March 10, 2020.

Berube, M. (2002). Going public: how the 'public intellectual' went from a buzzword to a relic, in one short decade. *Washington Post*, 7 July.

Black, T. (2021). Jordan Peterson: neither hero nor Hitler. *Spiked*, 19 March.

Blue, A. (1983). Agent provocateur of culture. *The Times*, 28 June.

Bowles, N. (2018). Jordan Peterson: custodian of the patriarchy. *New York Times*, 18 May.

Brooker, B. (2019). The 14 rules for eternal fascism: Jordan Peterson and the far right. *Overlord*, 14 February.

Brooks, M. (2020). *Against the web: a cosmopolitan answer to the new right*. Zero Books.

Burkeman, O. (2021). Beyond Order by Jordan Peterson review – more rules for life. *Guardian*, 2 March.

Burton, T.I. (2018). The religious hunger that drives Jordan Peterson's fandom. *Vox*, 1 June.

Bush, S. (2018). Bursting the bubble. *New Statesman*, 2 February, p. 21.

Coser, L. (1970). *Men of ideas*. Free Press.

Crews, F. (2018). *Freud: the making of an illusion*. Profile Books.

Cussen, J. (2022). Jordan Peterson's shadow: the postmodern neo-Marxism conspiracy theory. *The Living Philosophy*, 12 May.

Doidge, N. (2018). 'Preface' to Jordan Peterson, *12 rules for life: an antidote to chaos*. Penguin.

Driessens, O. (2013). Celebrity capital: redefining celebrity using field theory. *Theory and Society*, 2(5), 543–560.

Drezner, D. (2017). *The ideas industry: how pessimists, partisans, and plutocrats are transforming the marketplace of ideas*. Oxford University Press.

Eisenberg, D. (2008). Becoming Susan Sontag. *New York Review of Books*, 18 December.

Flanagan, C. (2018). Why is the left so afraid of Jordan Peterson? *The Atlantic*, 9 August.

Hamburger, J. (2018). The 'intellectual dark web' is nothing new. *Los Angeles Review of Books*, 18 July.

Hartman, A. (2019). *A war for the soul of America*. University of Chicago Press.

Hawley, G. (2018). *The alt-right: what everyone needs to know*. Oxford University Press.

Jacobs, R.N and Townsley, E. (2011). *The space of opinion: media intellectuals and the public sphere*. Oxford University Press.

Keren, M. and Hawkins, R. (eds) (2015). *Speaking power to truth: digital discourse and the public intellectual*. Athabasca University Press.

Kimmel, M. and Ferber, A.L. (2000). 'White men are this nation': right-wing militias and the restoration of rural American masculinity. *Rural Sociology*, 65(4), 582–604.

Kunzru, H. (2018). 12 Rules for Life by Jordan B. Peterson review. *Guardian*, 18 January, 08.59 GMT.

Lacayo, R. (2005). The sensuous intellectual. *Time Magazine*, 3 January.

Law, K. (2018). Jordan Peterson: an interview with the world famous 'anti-snowflake' crusader. *London Evening Standard*, 17 January.

Lewis, H. (2021). What happened to Jordan Peterson? *Atlantic*, 2 March.

Lumby, C. (1999). Genre anxiety in the postmodern public sphere. *Media International Australia*, 90(1), 1–210.

Lynskey, D. (2018). How dangerous is Jordan B. Peterson, the rightwing professor who 'hit a hornets' nest'? *Guardian*, 7 February.

MacDougald, P. (2018). Why they listen to Jordan Peterson. *New York Review of Books*, 11 February.

Mance, H. (2018). Jordan Peterson: one thing I'm not is naive. *Financial Times*, 1 June.

Mishra, P. (2018). Jordan Peterson and fascist mysticism. *New York Review of Books*, 19 March.

Moser, B. (2020). *Sontag: her life*. Penguin.

Nichols, T. (2017). *The death of expertise: the campaign against established knowledge and why it matters*. Oxford University Press.

Nisbet, M.C. (2014). Disruptive ideas: public intellectuals and their arguments for action on climate change. *WIREs Climate Change*, 5, 809–823.

Peterson, J.B. (1999). *Maps of meaning: the architecture of belief*. Routledge.

Peterson, J.B. (2018). *12 rules for life: an antidote to chaos*. Penguin.

Peterson, J.B. (2018). Interview with Helen Lewis. *GQ Magazine*, 18 October.

Peterson, J. B.(2021). *Beyond order: 12 more rules for life*. Penguin.

Peterson, J.B (2024) Bureaucrats will rue the day they tried to shut me up. *National Post*, 17 January.

Posner, R.A. (2001). *Decline of the public intellectuals: a study of decline*. Harvard University Press.

Quinne, A. (2018). Thought leaders: From foreign troll farms to Instagram models, countless forces are working to 'influence' our behavior. How will we know if they've succeeded? *New York Times*, 25 November.

Rajan, A. (2018). Uncommon sense. *New Statesman*, 2 September, 147(5405), 56.

Roberts, A. (2018). What can we learn from the Jordan Peterson phenomenon?

Robinson, N.J. (2018). The intellectual we deserve. *Current Affairs*, 14 March.

Rollyson, C. and Paddock, L. (2007). *Susan Sontag: the making of an icon*. W.W. Norton.

Said, E. (2002). The public role of writers and intellectuals. In Small, H. (ed.), *The public intellectual*. Blackwell.

Shea, C. (2014). The new academic celebrity: why a different kind of scholar—and idea—hits big today *Chronicle of Higher Education*, 60(31), 18 April.

Spears. T. (2017). How controversial U of T prof Jordan Peterson became a lightning rod. *Ottawa Citizen*, 10 March.

Stedman Jones, G. (2017). *Karl Marx: greatness and illusion*. Penguin.

Weiss, B. (2018). Meet the renegades of the intellectual dark web. *New York Times*, 8 May.

Whiting, A. and Williams, D. (2013). Why people use social media: a uses and gratifications approach. *Qualitative Market Research: An International Journal*, 16(4), 362–369.

Yang, W. (2018). The passion of Jordan Peterson. *Esquire*, 1 May.

Žižek, S. (2018). Why do people find Jordan Peterson so convincing? *Independent*, 13 February.

# THE FUTURE OF CULTS
## FROM QANON TO THE CULT OF AI

### WHEN PROPHESIES FAIL

In October 2017, an anonymous internet user shared a series of posts on the message board 4chan. The user claimed to be disclosing government secrets and military intelligence to awaken people to evil threats facing the world, signing off with the pseudonym 'Q' – a signifier of their 'Q Clearance' access to restricted US national security data. Q's posts – referred to as 'Q drops' – were strategically written in a cryptic language and required decoding to decipher the military intelligence concealed in them. The QAnon movement circulated on the fringes of rightwing internet culture for years before becoming more visible and mainstream in 2020 following the outbreak of the coronavirus pandemic. Thousands of Q drops (referred to as breadcrumbs) were posted on a series of message boards (4Chan/8Chan/8Kun) over a three-year period between October 2017 to December 2020, reemerging briefly in June 2022 after a two-year hiatus. The internet made the movement highly participatory, with Anons (adherents) actively collaborating online to decode posts in a decentralised mode of crowdsourced storytelling. Much of the discourse around QAnon is conspiratorial, premised on the foundational belief that society is controlled by the 'Deep State': a global cabal of Satan-worshipping paedophiles comprised of Democrats, Hollywood celebrities and billionaires, who control politics, entertainment and the media, and are believed to engage in human trafficking and sacrifice their victims to harvest a life-extending chemical called adrenochrome.

The movement coalesces around cult idioms and motifs – such as 'Where We Go One, We Go All' – and assumes a *religious* dimension by providing a framework to comprehend the problem of evil: job loss, child trafficking, social inequality and the pandemic (Argentino, 2023). True believers cast former US President Donald Trump as a 'lightworker' fighting the Deep State in a grand battle between good and evil with Anons called upon by Q and QAnon influencers to participate as 'digital soldiers' in an information war online in order to save humanity. The religiosity of QAnon is built upon the *revelation* of concealed or oppressed truths; it is *disruptive,* holding that liberty and truth can only be achieved by the disciplined annihilation of the fortified positions that uphold popular consciousness of paramount reality.

The QAnon movement was energised by a series of failed predictions. Q occupied the role of a prophet, a visionary with access to secret knowledge and special insight about the future. True believers of QAnon forecast that Hillary Clinton's arrest was imminent, that John F. Kennedy Jr. would return (two decades after his death) as Donald Trump's Vice President when the former president was reinstated and that a civil war would ensue. These predictions were subsets of two principal prophesies. (1) the Storm – a violent day of reckoning involving the mass arrest and execution of thousands of corrupt, evil Deep State actors who will be brought to justice for their crimes; (2) The Great Awakening – a global shift in consciousness in which people realise the corruption of these global elites and society will enter a utopian age. Neither prediction came to pass, but this did not alter the convictions of true believers. Although Q consistently made predictions that failed to eventuate, true believers continuously adapted their narratives to account for inconsistencies. For example, during the climactic January 6 Capitol insurrection, some QAnon followers claimed that, despite having lost the US presidential election, former US President Donald Trump would be elected for a second term on 20 January 2021. The date was prophesied as a day of reckoning when Trump, together with the support of the US military, would declare martial law and begin implementing 'The Storm' – a plan to arrest and execute Democrat leaders. When these predictions failed to materialise, some true believers revised the date of their predictions of Trump's re-inauguration to 4 March 2021. When that date proved uneventful, it was revised again to 20 March 2021, which also failed to eventuate. Despite these setbacks and disappointments, QAnon channels and influencers continued to create content promoting the movement (McDonald, 2021; Sommer, 2023); the denial of institutional evidence in place of secret knowledge characteristic of cult formation.

The ideological fervor expressed by QAnon adherents in light of conflicting events is characteristic of how cults respond to disconfirmed expectations. In the classic text *When Prophecy Fails* (1956), Leon Festinger, Henry Riecken and Stanley Schachter studied how groups of believers coped when their prophetic expectations were disconfirmed. The researchers introduced the term 'cognitive dissonance' to describe beliefs and behaviours inconsistent (dissonant) with each other (Festinger at al., 1956: 25–26). Their research on cognitive dissonance demonstrated that each compromise and act of commitment made by a believer made it more difficult to admit that they have been deceived (Festinger et al., 1956). A belief will, therefore, be resistant to change if it has been enacted through behaviour. For example, if one believes a prediction in the second coming of Christ where sinners will be doomed and the good will be saved, they will act according to that belief (Festinger et al., 1956). As a result, even if the prophesised event fails to materialise on the predicted date, disconfirmation of messiahship is unlikely to daunt their belief. On the contrary, committed followers tend to experience renewed confidence in their beliefs, enacting a familiar pattern: 'recovery of conviction, followed by new heights of enthusiasm and proselytising' (Festinger et al., 1956). This pattern is not limited to religious cults. Cognitive dissonance was evident in much of the conspiratorial discourse that circulated during the pandemic from COVID denialism (theories that COVID is a hoax, the virus does not exist or it is just like the flu) to anti-vaccinationists who predicted varied and conflicting harmful consequences of vaccination ranging from infertility to depopulation and surveillance. As conceptualised by Festinger et al.'s (1956) work on cognitive dissonance, the failure of these predictions resulted in renewed fanaticism and confidence in the anti-vaccination movement. In many respects, they are living out Samuel Beckett's exhortation: 'Ever tried. Ever failed. No matter. Try again. Fail again. Fail better.'

## THICK AND THIN CULTS: THE SPECTRUM OF CULTIC INFLUENCE

QAnon is a timely case study for the topic of cults not least because it complicates and expands the notion of what constitutes a cult in the twenty-first century. Although the QAnon movement mobilised offline in conventions, protests and real-word violence, it is primarily an online movement. True believers are highly networked online, collectively decoding Q drops and contributing to a decentralised narrative. While QAnon influencers amplify the movement online, QAnon does not adhere to a visible hierarchical structure as is typical of a cult. Instead, it adopts a molecular form of organisation. There are different subsets and variations of QAnon on different platforms (for example, what is termed 'pastel QAnon' on the photo-video sharing app, Instagram – Argentino, 2021). Moreover, whereas cults are traditionally led by a single messianic figure, there is a no clear leadership in QAnon, with questions remaining about whether the anonymous 'Q' is a single poster or a team of posters helping Trump to take down the evil Deep State. As a result, there is a lack of consensus among cult researchers around whether QAnon is a conspiracy theory, a new religious movement, a cult or a terrorist group (see Amarasingam et al., 2023; Juergensmeyer, 2022; Stein, 2022). The possibility of leaderless cults or decentralised cults online complicates traditional understandings of what constitutes a cult and how the leadership, structure and ideologies of a cult are used to control members.

The ways in which online cultic groups like QAnon provide the conditions for conversion and coercion to take place also differ from offline cults. People are recruited into cults for a variety of reasons. Some people are born into cults and others are recruited or coerced into them (usually with a lack of informed consent as a result of deception and undue influence). The social and psychological process of conversion is commonly described as brainwashing, thought reform, coercive persuasion, radicalisation, grooming and mind control (see Hassan, 2015; Lifton, 2012; Singer, 1996; Stein, 2022). Cults control what people do with their bodies and resources (time, energy, wealth). The coercive mechanisms of online cults are more difficult to enforce than offline cults. Despite attempts by cults to encourage members to self-isolate from friends and family, it is more challenging to separate a member online from their social networks than it is offline if they are physically isolated in a remote setting or commune, such as Jonestown. Online cults tend to rely on influence, repetition and propaganda to encourage conversion and commitment from their followers. The internet has contributed to what we have described as a cultic moment. The ubiquity of digital technologies, social media and message boards provides a platform for like-minded users to assemble and for conversion and coercion to take place. People today are able to connect, share ideas and mobilise online. The technological affordances of digital technologies create new opportunities to network that were not available in the age of legacy media. However, as documented by our case studies, there are numerous pathways to radicalisation and violent extremism, and online exposure to cultic influence does not guarantee conversion or radicalisation.

Cults exist on a spectrum from relatively benign to those that exert exploitative control and undue influence (Hassan and Shah, 2019; Hassan, 2020). Traditional understandings of religious cults and doomsday cults have been challenged and complicated by new forms of cultic influence that permeate social relations in the twenty-first century. Thick and thin cults share some characteristics: charismatic, authoritarian leaders, transcendent belief systems that provide answers to life's most pressing questions, systems of influence and control comprised of specific rules and regulations (Lalich, 2004). The techniques and tactics cults use to establish influence may vary, but most cults employ tactics of subterfuge and coercive persuasion to control their followers. Despite the overlap between thick and thin cults, it would be a mistake to conflate the two. The six case studies featured in this book explore messianic cults in different historical and cultural contexts. While there is overlap in the characteristics of cultic influence, it would be an oversimplification to equate the Cult of Celebrity or the Cult of the Entrepreneur with a Doomsday Cult. What these cults share in common are important social and psychological functions which they promise seekers. As exemplified in Chapter 2, these include the promise of:

1. meaning and purpose;
2. identity and belonging;
3. knowledge and truth;
4. feeling and connection;
5. leadership and guidance.

Despite the recurring conditions that give rise to cults over time, there have been significant changes to the structure of cults in the twenty-first century. Whereas some contemporary messianic figures analysed in this book lead cults that adhere to a hierarchical structure (e.g. Andrew Tate), other figures achieve cult followings online as part of a network of online influencers proselytising about a common cause. Figures such as Jordan B. Peterson, for example, establish charismatic authority and a loyal following, but they do not lead a cult in the traditional sense of a group bound by a hierarchical structure and coercive control. Instead, Peterson, like many other influencers who achieve cult-like followings online, is part of a network of like-minded figures who position themselves as anti-establishment and cross-promote each other's brands. These networked groups of cultic influence resemble the anti-vaccine movement comprised of a series of high-profile influencers with cult followings, who network with other anti-vaccine advocates to broaden their reach and influence and monetise their brands (Baker et al., 2023; Baker and Walsh, 2023; 2024). With the ubiquity of AI, personalised chat bots and virtual influencers on the horizon, we can expect new forms of cultic influence to emerge, which integrate technology and popular cultural artefacts into a spiritual framework. These are not traditional cults in the religious sense, but what Adam Possamai (2005) refers to as a 'hyper-real religion': 'a simulacrum of a religion created out of, or in symbiosis with, commodified popular culture which provides inspiration at a metaphorical level and/or is a source of beliefs for everyday life' (Possamai, 2012: 20; see also Argentino, 2023).

## THE CULTIC MOMENT

We live in what we have referred to as a cultic moment. That is, a historical juncture in which low trust relations are attached to the central institutions of normative order and a sense of exhaustion with the dominant beliefs, practices and associations of the past prevail. An adjunct of this which is propitious to the multiplication of cults is the widespread rejection of complexity and its replacement with a search for simple solutions to complex social, cultural, economic and political problems (Baker et al., 2023). It is impossible to estimate the number of cults globally, given that they range from Scientology to fitness cults and cult brands. The cultic moment is symptomatic of low intuitional trust and de-traditionalisation, both of which encourage seekers to yearn for new authorities to give meaning and direction to life. The cultic moment also speaks to the existential loneliness and despair many people feel in late modern life, a sense of meaningless combined with the desperate need to belong. The cult followings of Ye (Kanye West), Andrew Tate and Jordan B. Peterson reflect the fact that these figures offer an antidote to many young men's feelings of existential despair. The internet enables these figures to attract followers at an unprecedented speed and scale. It also provides new opportunities to achieve influence online with transgressive opinions and performative displays used to garner attention and monetise eyeballs (see Chapters 6 and 7). In the current attention economy and digital environment, strategic cross-promotion and micro-targeting functions as a form of recruitment, with users algorithmically turned into consumers as they are steered to motivational, aspirational and outrageous content.

It is easy to dismiss true believers as irrational and delusional. What this misses are the important functions that cults play in a post-traditional society. Cults provide their members with *meaning and purpose* and a reason to believe and trust in something greater than themselves. In so doing they provide a transcendental antidote to what Zygmunt Bauman (2013) describes as 'liquid modernity.' Cults provide their members with sense of *identity and belonging*. They offer members an exclusive in-group identity that casts the world into good and bad actors, light and dark forces, those who know the truth and those who do not. Consequently, they provide a religious framework to understand the problem of evil and one's place in the world (Argentino, 2023; Baker et al., 2023). Cults provide their members with *knowledge and truth*. They claim to have access to a privileged epistemology and ontology, which provides the assurance of certitude as an antidote to a climate of fear, distrust and uncertainty. Cults foster a sense of *feeling and connection*. They establish and sustain strong emotional attachments to cult leaders, members and the ideals of the group by participating in collective rituals and practices. Cults provide *leadership and guidance*. They are characteristically directed by visionary leaders, who profess to have exceptional qualities, bestow exclusive 'truths' and convictions and guide members towards 'the light.' Digital technologies provide the capacity for leaderless cults with loosely defined hierarchies to emerge. But cults could not exist without tapping into a wider, shared sense of vulnerability and idealism. Andrew Tate's bleak vision of the average man's plight speaks to the Sisyphean struggle to find meaning and purpose in life. Condemned to repeat the same meaningless tasks overtime, 'The struggle itself towards the heights is enough to fill a man's heart. One must imagine Sisyphus happy' (Camus, 1942).

## REFERENCES

Amarasingam, A., Argentino, M.-A., Johnston, D. and Mosurinjohn, S. (2023). Categorizing QAnon. *The Social Science of QAnon: A New Social and Political Phenomenon* (p. 271). Cambridge University Press.

Argentino, M-A. (2021). Pastel QAnon. *Global Network on Extremism and Technology*. https://gnet-research.org/2021/03/17/pastel-qanon/

Argentino, M-A. (2023). *QAnon: A survey of the evolution of the movement from conspiracy theory to new religious movement*. Doctoral dissertation, Concordia University.

Baker, S.A., McLaughlin, E. and Rojek, C. (2023). Simple solutions to wicked problems: cultivating true believers of anti-vaccine conspiracies during the COVID-19 pandemic. *European Journal of Cultural Studies*. doi: 13675494231173536.

Baker, S.A. and Walsh, M.J. (2023). 'A mother's intuition: it's real and we have to believe in it': how the maternal is used to promote vaccine refusal on Instagram. *Information, Communication & Society*, 26(8), 1675–1692.

Baker, S.A. and Walsh, M.J. (2024). 'Memes save lives': stigma and the production of anti-vaccination memes during the COVID-19 pandemic. *Social Media + Society*, 10(1).

Bauman, Z. (2013). *Liquid modernity*. John Wiley & Sons.

Camus, A. (1942). *Le mythe du Sisyphe* [The myth of Sisyphus]. Gallimard.

Festinger, L. Riecken, H.W. and Schachter, S. ([1956] 2013). *When prophecy fails: a classic study*. Simon and Schuster.

Hassan, S. (2015). *Combating cult mind control: the #1 best-selling guide to protection, rescue, and recovery from destructive cults*. Freedom of Mind Press.

Hassan, S.A. (2020). The BITE model of authoritarian control: undue influence, thought reform, brainwashing, mind control, trafficking and the law. Doctoral dissertation, Fielding Graduate University.

Hassan, S.A. and Shah, M.J. (2019). The anatomy of undue influence used by terrorist cults and traffickers to induce helplessness and trauma, so creating false identities. *Ethics, Medicine and Public Health*, 8, 97–107.

Juergensmeyer, M. (2022). QAnon as religious terrorism. *Journal of Religion and Violence*, 10(1), 89–100.

Lalich, J. (2004). *Bounded choice: true believers and charismatic cults*. University of California Press.

Lifton, R.J. (2012). *Thought reform and the psychology of totalism: a study of 'brainwashing' in China*. UNC Press Books.

McDonald, B. (2021). *How QAnon reacts to failed predictions*. Global Network of Extremism and Technology.

Possamai, A. (2005). *Religion and popular culture: a hyper-real testament* (No. 7). Peter Lang.

Possamai, A. (ed.) (2012). *Handbook of hyper-real religions* (Vol. 5). Brill.

Singer, M.T. (1996). Therapy, thought reform, and cults. *Transactional Analysis Journal*, 26(1), 15–22.

Sommer, W. (2023) *Trust the plan: the rise of QAnon and the conspiracy that unhinged America*. HarperCollins.

Stein, A. (2021). *Terror, love and brainwashing: attachment in cults and totalitarian systems*. Routledge.

Stein, A. (2022). *Political cults and the use of cultic tactics in the recruitment and mobilisation of participants in the January 6 attack on the Capitol*. Select Committee to Investigate the January 6th Attack on the United States Capitol. Available at: https://www.alexandrastein.com/uploads/2/8/0/1/28010027/select_cmte_on_jan_6_statement_for_the_record_a_stein.pdf

# SUBJECT INDEX

affiliate marketing 115, 118
algorithm 9, 112, 114, 147
American Dream 91, 97, 104, 119
anti-cult movement 12, 60
Apple, Inc. 22, 83–4, 86–92
apocalypse: 3–4, 35–6, 61, 98; apocalypticism 46–9; apocalyptic race war 55–7, 63
artificial intelligence (AI) 19, 83, 115
aspirational lifestyle 97, 108, 112, 147
attention capital 69, 72–3, 78
attention economy 111–2, 147
attention hacking 96, 112
audacity 76–7, 79
authenticity 19, 94, 96, 98, 126

Beach Boys 53–4, 56, 58, 62; *see also* Wilson, D.
Beatles 53, 55–7, 62–3
Beckett, S. 143
bespoke aggregation 75–6
Bitcoin 117
Blockchain 117
Book of Revelation 36, 39–40, 47
bounded choice 105, 120–1; *see also* Lalich
Branch Davidians 9, 32–45; *see also* Koresh, D.
brand 3, 13–4, 20–8, 64, 70, 77, 82–4, 88–102, 107, 112–5, 118–120, 126, 146–7; *see also* cult brand and personal brand
brainwashing 12, 24, 29, 60, 121–2, 142, 148–9

cargo cults 2–3, 11
cease to exist 54, 56, 66
celebrity: 8–9, 13, 21, 60–3, 67–81, 93, 125, 133–4, 145; achieved celebrity 67, 74; ascribed celebrity 67; celetoid 67; *see also* microcelebrity
celebrity culture 62, 70–1, 73–4, 79–80
charisma 3–7, 13, 17, 22, 35, 46, 51, 60, 67–8, 78, 99, 105, 110, 124, 135–6, 145–6
Christian Science 104
clergy 34
climate crisis 48, 135
coercion 12, 22–7, 99, 111, 118, 136, 144–5
cognitive dissonance 143
consciousness 7, 15, 17, 20–2, 34, 63, 67–73, 77–8, 87, 124–5, 131, 142
conspiracy theory 35, 75, 97–9, 117, 121–2, 125, 135, 137, 144
conversion 22–7, 46, 54, 111,118, 144–5; *see also* radicalisation
coronavirus pandemic 96–7, 141–3
counterculture 4, 20–1, 50, 52, 62–3, 87–9, 92, 106, 109

creed 12, 34, 36, 56
cult brand 13, 27; *see also* brand
cultic experience 14–18
cult of celebrity 67–81, 145
cult of the entrepreneur 8–9, 82–102, 145
cult of the public intellectual 9, 123–40
cult of personality 21, 46, 73
cultic milieu 7–8, 33, 44–8, 50–1, 61
cultic moment 6–9, 14,18–21, 33, 44, 60, 78–9,145–8
cultification 35, 41–4
cults: definition 4–9, 12–22, 32–4, 47–9, 67–71, 82–6, 103–6, 123–5; origins 34–5, 49–50, 71–3, 86–91, 106–9, 125–7; maintenance 35–40, 50–60, 73–7, 91–7, 109–118, 127–35; futures 40–4, 60–3, 77–80, 97–9, 118–20, 135–7; *see also* religious cults; doomsday cults, the cult of celebrity, the cult of the entrepreneur, self-help cults and the cult of the public intellectual
culture wars 125, 128–9

Death Valley 55–6
detraditionalisation 6, 14, 19, 44, 147; *see also* Giddens, A.
Deep State 141–2, 144,
Doomsday Clock 47
doomsday cults 8–9, 20, 22–3, 46–66, 145

elites 16, 35, 40, 96, 106, 117, 142
Emerson, R. W. 104
End Times 46–8, 55–6
entrepreneur 113; *see also* cult of the entrepreneur
expertise 17, 19, 88, 124; *see also* experts
experts 16, 106; *see also* expertise
extremism 23, 40, 98, 145

far-right 4, 23, 96, 112
feminism 106, 108

followership 17–8, 36–8, 50–2, 60, 67, 74, 78, 91–2, 94–9, 105–10, 113–6, 130, 133–5

Gates, B. 84
gospel 53–4, 130–2, 135–6
Great Reset 137; *see also* conspiracy theories
grooming 39, 53–4, 69, 89, 116, 144
group dynamics 46, 117, 120
guru 6–7, 9, 13–4, 46–50, 52–3, 55, 58, 63, 82, 94, 103–11, 114, 117–20, 136

health 22–3, 26, 94, 104, 106, 108, 110, 112, 118, 120
Helter Skelter 46, 55–7, 60, 62
Holmes, E. 83–6, 90

idealism 48
ideology 3, 26, 105, 108
idols 1–2, 9, 67
Iman 1, 5
incels 108; *see also* manosphere and red pill
Intellectual Dark Web 3, 128–30
ISIS 1–2

Jesus Christ 5, 50–1, 58
Jihad 1–5
Jobs, S. 84–6, 88, 91–2; *see also* Apple Inc.
Jones, A. 75, 112

Koresh, D. 32–45; *see also* Branch Davidians

language 21–2, 53, 60, 71, 83, 132, 141
LaBianca murders 57–8, 61, 63
Large Group Awareness Trainings (LGAT) 110
law of attraction 104, 114
liberalism 104, 106
libertarian 97, 136
love bombing 12
luxury 32, 57, 70, 108, 113, 115, 118

## SUBJECT INDEX

manifestation 34–5, 53, 78
manosphere 9, 108
Manson, C. 9, 46–66; Manson Family 46–66; Mansonism 61; Mansonites 60–3
Marian cult 34
masculinity 107–9, 112–3, 116, 119–20, 131
Matrix 117–8, 120
meritocracy 97–8
messianic leader 2–9, 14, 22, 27, 37–8, 41–2, 44
microcelebrity 94–99
microcultures 19, 21–2
Microsoft 84; *see also* Gates, B.
micro–targeting 147
Millerism 35
Mill, J. S. 104
mindset 49, 54, 112–5
motivation 25, 114, 134, 147
murder 22, 38, 48, 51, 55–9
Musk, E. 9, 48, 82–102, 115

New Age 21, 106, 108, 114
New Thought 104
NXIVM 110–1

Paltrow, G. 112
patriarchy 35, 123, 131
personal brand 93, 96, 98
personal responsibility 112, 116, 131–2
Peterson, J. B. 112, 123–40
podcast 3, 63, 93, 126, 130
Polanski, R. 57, 62
populism 18, 43, 117, 120
profane 1, 17, 110
prophesy 47–8, 55
proselytising 54, 120, 143, 146
public intellectual 8–9, 123–40

QAnon 4–5, 34–5, 43, 141–4

radicalisation 4, 23, 48, 55, 128, 144–5; *see also* conversion
rapture culture 47

recruitment 2, 24, 33–4, 40, 46, 54, 109, 111, 118, 147
red pill 108, 117, 129
religion 5–6, 9, 13, 22, 32–4, 36, 40, 47, 58, 72, 75, 78, 90, 106, 119, 127, 146
religious cults 8–9, 23, 32–45, 110, 143, 145
religious fundamentalism 4
remnant religion 36
rites of passage 55
rituals 2, 5, 17, 25, 33, 147
Robbins, T. 110, 114
Rogan, J. 3

sacred 17, 34, 53, 110
salvation 15, 18–9, 34–5, 76, 79, 82, 97, 106, 120, 127, 130–3, 136–7
scandal 19, 98, 108
Scientology 50, 110–1, 147
sects 5, 32–8, 41–3
self-actualisation 106, 109
self-discovery 120
self-help 14–5, 106, 126, 130, 134, 136; *see also* self-help cults and self-improvement
self-help cults 8–9, 103–121
self-improvement 15, 103, 106–7, 109–11
self-made 97, 113; *see also* American Dream and social mobility
self-mastery 119
self-reliance 103–4, 132
self-transformation 24, 109–10, 120, 136
Seventh Day Adventists 35–7
sexual exploitation 38, 52–5
Silicon Valley 83–91, 93, 97, 130
social media 9, 14, 19, 23, 27, 44, 93–9, 107–8, 111–5, 126–7, 129–30, 133–6, 145
social mobility 104, 113; *see also* self-made
social movements 6–7, 95, 124
Smiles, S. 103–4, 119

Sontag, S. 123–5
Spahn Movie Ranch 52, 55–6, 60
spirituality 21, 92, 106, 108; *see also* New Age
subcultures 20–2, 50, 92, 112
Summer of Love 62–3
surveillance 12, 126, 143

Tate, A. 103–22, 146–8
Tate, S.: murder 57, 63; Tate-LaBianca murder trial 58–9, 61; Tate family 61
Tesla, Inc. 48, 83, 85, 93, 96
transcendent 15, 21, 34, 44, 50, 79, 90, 103, 105–6, 120, 125, 131, 145, 147

trolls 97, 99, 112
Trump, D. 43, 77, 9–6, 98, 111–2, 142, 144

vulnerability 24, 110, 148

Waco 35–44
wealth creation 53–5, 78, 83, 104, 106, 108, 110–20, 144
wellness 75, 94, 120
West, K. (Ye) 9, 67–81, 147
White Album, Beatles 55–6, 59
Wilson, D. (Beach Boys) 53–6, 58; *see also* Beach Boys
Winfrey O. 107–8
World Economic Forum 137

# AUTHOR INDEX

Acosta, P. M. 13, 27, 91, 99
Adorno, T. 71, 79
Alexander, J. 124, 132, 137
Alison, L. 49, 64
Amarasingam, A. 144, 148
Argentino, M-A. 142, 144, 146–8
Arnold, J. 38, 45
Astor, M. 76, 80
Aupers, S. 6, 10

Bainbridge, W. 4, 5, 11, 32
Baker, S. A. 6–10, 13, 16–19, 27, 87, 93–9, 104, 106–7, 110–2, 117, 120–1, 146–8
Barbour, K. 69, 80
Barker, E. 49, 64
Barkun, M. 15–6, 27, 41, 45
Bauman, Z. 16, 28, 147–8
Becker, H. 40–1, 45
Belk, R. 27–8, 86, 89, 91–2, 99
Bell, D. 6, 10
Berger, A. 4, 10
Bohm, J. 49, 64
Boorstin, D. 70–1, 79–80, 92, 99
Bourdieu, P. 20, 28
boyd, d. 71, 79, 81, 95, 99
Bueno, B.J. 13–4, 20, 26–7, 30, 91–2, 98, 101
Bugliosi, V. 46, 51, 56–60, 62, 64

Calhoun, C. 78, 80
Campbell, C. 7, 10, 33, 45
Camus, A. 148
Chen, C. 90, 100
Cicarrello-Maher, G. 77, 80
Clancy, B. 3, 10
Conway, F. 56, 64
Coppleston, F. 34, 45
Coser, L. 123, 132, 138

Deutschman, A. 86, 91, 100
Devasagayam, R. 13, 27, 91, 99
Didion, J. 46, 62, 64
Driessens, O. 72, 80, 126, 138
Du Bois, W. 77, 80
Duffy B. E. 94, 100
Durkheim, E. 17, 28, 110

Eco, U. 47, 64
Emmons, N. 46, 50, 52, 56–7, 60–1, 64

Ferrari Braun, A. 91, 93, 100
Festinger, L. 47, 64, 143, 148
Franck, G. 69, 80
Freud, S. 117, 121, 123
Furl, K. 10, 23, 29

Gamson, J. 71, 79–80
Gaonkar, D. 78, 80
Gentry, C. 46, 51, 56–60, 62, 64

## Author Index

George, C. 76, 80
Giddens, A. 6, 10, 19, 28, 106, 121
Goffman, E. 117, 121
Gomez, M. 76
Gordon, B. 32, 45
Gramsci, A. 8, 10
Guinn, J. 39, 42, 45, 47, 61, 64

Hassan, S. 12–3, 21, 24, 27–8, 110, 121, 144–5, 148
Houtman, D. 6, 10

Ingram, M. 29, 106, 121
Isaacson, W. 10, 85–6, 100

Jansen, W. 34, 45
Jurgensmeyer, M. 4, 10

Kahney, L. 92, 100
Kelly, K. 88, 100
King, B. 70, 80

Lalich, J. 4, 10, 13, 20, 22–4, 29, 105, 109–10, 118, 120–1, 144, 149
Leary, T. 52, 65
Levy, S. 89, 101
Lewis, R. 94, 96, 101, 112, 121
Lifton, R. J. 12–3, 24, 29, 46–9, 65, 144, 149
Lofland, J. 25, 29, 46, 48, 65
Lofton, K. 77, 80
Lorenz, T. 95, 101
Lowenthal, L. 71, 80
Lumby, C. 125, 139

MacDonald, A. 45
Macmillen, S. 35, 45
McGee, M. 107, 119, 121
McLaughlin, E. 19, 28, 87, 101, 148
Marcus, S. 71, 73, 80
Marshall, P. D. 48, 65, 69, 80
Martin, D. 21, 29, 40–1, 44–5

Marwick, A. 4, 10, 23, 29, 71, 79, 81–4, 88–9, 93–4, 96–8, 101, 112, 121
Monk-Payton, B. 75, 77, 81
Montell, A. 4, 10, 21, 30, 53, 65
Moore, C. 69, 80
Murray, D. 3, 10

Newport, K. 36–42, 45
Niebhur, R. 33
Notermans, C. 34, 45

Phillips, W. 9–10, 96, 101, 112, 122
Pierini, D. 92, 100
Pope, L. 78, 81
Possamai, A. 146, 149
Postman, N. 70–1, 79, 81

Qutb, S. 1–2, 5, 10

Ragas, M.W. 13–4, 20, 26–7, 30, 91–2, 98, 101
Rambo, L. R. 22, 25–6, 30
Richardson, C. 77, 81
Richardson, J. 25, 30, 33, 45
Riecken, H.W. 28, 64, 143, 149
Rojek, C. 6–7, 9–10, 13, 16–19, 27, 75, 81, 93–4, 97, 99, 106–7, 110–2, 121, 148
Rush, T. 35, 45
Rushkoff, 48, 65

Sanders, E. 47, 50, 52, 57–8, 66
Schachter, S. 28, 64, 143, 149
Sedgwick, M. 3, 11
Siegelman, J. 56, 64
Singer, M. T. 12–3, 30, 144, 149
Smiles, S. 103–4, 119,
Sommer, W. 143, 149
Stark, R. 4–5, 11, 22, 25
Stein, A. 12, 110, 122, 144, 149
Strauss, N. 114, 122

Taylor, C. 78, 80
Taylor, K. 13, 30
Teitelbaum, B. 3, 11

Thiel, P. 84, 93, 102
Thompson, J. B. 19, 30, 47, 66
Thrower, J. 34, 45
Thunberg, G. 48, 66
Toobin, J. 38, 43, 45
Troeltsch, E. 32, 45
Trueman, C. 33, 45
Tumbat, G. 27–8, 86, 89, 91–2, 99
Turchin, P. 3, 11
Turner, F. 20, 30, 87–8, 95, 99, 102

Vaynerchuk, G. 93, 102
Vidal, G. 62, 66
Voltaire 9, 11

Watson, C. 47, 53–7, 66
Weber, M. 7, 11, 17, 31, 67–8, 81
Weiss, B. 3, 11, 130
Westerkamp, M. 35, 45
Wilson, B. 68, 78, 81
Wolfe, T. 89–90, 102

For Product Safety Concerns and Information please contact our EU representative GPSR@taylorandfrancis.com
Taylor & Francis Verlag GmbH, Kaufingerstraße 24, 80331 München, Germany

www.ingramcontent.com/pod-product-compliance
Lightning Source LLC
Chambersburg PA
CBHW071821230426
43670CB00013B/2527